the
READING
coach 2

MORE TOOLS AND STRATEGIES
FOR STUDENT-FOCUSED COACHES

Jan Hasbrouck, Ph.D.
Carolyn Denton, Ph.D.

Sopris West®
EDUCATIONAL SERVICES

A Cambium Learning® Company

BOSTON, MA • LONGMONT, CO

Printed in the United States of America
Published and Distributed by

Sopris West®
EDUCATIONAL SERVICES

A Cambium Learning® Company

4093 Specialty Place • Longmont, Colorado 80504
(303) 651-2829 • www.sopriswest.com

(178861/332/02-09)

To my children, Isaac Spinell and Lizzey Spinell,
who have enriched my life more than words can express.
~ JEH

To my grandchild, Bella Vaca, who is learning to read
and who brings joy to my life every day.
~ CAD

ACKNOWLEDGMENTS

We would like to thank the hundreds of Reading Coaches who have attended our training sessions and workshops over the years. They have been invaluable in helping us shape and expand our Student-Focused Coaching model.

We would also like to thank the Coaches who have participated in research on our coaching approach, especially Jennifer Hocker, Vanessa Dainton, Carolyn Buss, Melinda McGrath, and fellow researcher Dr. Patricia Mathes.

ABOUT THE AUTHORS

Jan Hasbrouck, Ph.D., is an educational consultant, trainer, and researcher. She recently served as the executive consultant to the Washington State Reading Initiative. Dr. Hasbrouck worked as a reading specialist for 15 years before becoming a professor at the University of Oregon and later at Texas A&M University. She consults with schools, districts, and state departments of education with a focus on improving instruction for students who struggle with reading. Dr. Hasbrouck works with educators across the United States as well as internationally, helping teachers and administrators design and implement effective assessment and instructional programs targeted to help low-performing readers.

Dr. Hasbrouck earned her B.A. and M.A. from the University of Oregon and completed her Ph.D. at Texas A&M University. Her research in areas of reading fluency, reading assessment, coaching and consultation, and second-language learners has been published in numerous professional books and journals. Dr. Hasbrouck is the coauthor of *The Reading Coach: A How-To Manual for Success, Differentiated Instruction: Grouping for Success,* and several assessment tools. She is an author of MacMillan/McGraw-Hill's *Treasures* and *Triumphs* reading programs.

Carolyn Denton, Ph.D., is an educational consultant and a researcher at the Children's Learning Institute, part of the department of pediatrics at the University of Texas Health Science Center at Houston. Her work is focused on identifying and providing intervention to students with reading difficulties and disabilities and on the role of the Reading Coach.

A former reading teacher, Dr. Denton is committed to developing and evaluating interventions and professional development approaches that are effective and practical for schools to implement. Although much of her work has been in elementary schools, Dr. Denton recently led the Texas Adolescent Literacy Project, in which she and her team developed a schoolwide reading intervention approach for middle school and produced professional development materials for middle-school teachers working with struggling readers.

Dr. Denton has consulted with numerous state departments of education as well as educators and researchers across the U.S. and in Hong Kong, providing information and professional development related to reading instruction and coaching. She is a lead researcher and collaborator on several federally funded projects, including the Texas Center for Learning Disabilities, a research center funded by the National Institute for Child Health and Human Development. The work of Dr. Denton and her colleagues has been recognized by the International Reading Association, which awarded them the 2006 Albert J. Harris Award for a research article that made a significant contribution to the understanding of reading difficulties.

Dr. Denton is the author of *Responsive Reading Instruction,* a first-grade reading intervention program, and coauthor of *The Reading Coach: A How-To Manual for Success* as well as numerous articles and book chapters.

CONTENTS

Chapter 3: Problem Solving Within SFC

Chapter 4: Designing Academic Interventions for Students With Reading Difficulties

Chapter 5: Collaborative Planning for Student Behavior Concerns

Chapter 6: Student-Focused Classroom Observations

Chapter 7: Engaging Reluctant Teachers

1

OVERVIEW OF STUDENT-FOCUSED COACHING (SFC)

A rapidly growing number of professional educators are being asked to take on a new, important, challenging, and too-often vaguely defined role as a Reading Coach.* When we wrote our first book about coaching—*The Reading Coach: A How-To Manual for Success* (Hasbrouck & Denton, 2005, which we will call *The Reading Coach* book from here on)—we hoped we would provide some helpful guidance to teacher colleagues who were being asked to serve as Reading Coaches as well as to administrators who would be supervising and supporting them. In the ensuing years, we have had the privilege of working with many hundreds of Coaches and administrators who used the first book to help them successfully develop and implement coaching services. The purpose of this second book is to share some additional ideas and strategies for effective coaching.

In this chapter, we

- start with an overview of the roles of the Reading Coach, revisiting briefly the *why,* the *who,* and the *what* of coaching;
- examine different models of coaching; and
- reiterate the key role that administrators play in successful coaching.

The remaining chapters of this book provide some tools and strategies as well as ideas related to the *how* of successful coaching that add to and expand upon our first book.

Why Coaching?

The growing body of well-conducted, scientifically based research in the area of reading has provided both inspiration and a road map for how we should be helping students with reading. The inspiration comes from the many studies that have documented—again and again—

---

* Although there are many terms being used for educators who serve in this role, we will use the term "Reading Coach" (or, simply, the abbreviated term "Coach") in this book, as we did in our original book on this topic: *The Reading Coach: A How-To Manual for Success* (Hasbrouck & Denton, 2005).

that, with early intervention and sustained systematic, explicit, and intensive instruction across the grades, most reading difficulties can be prevented. It is also inspirational to know that is it never too late to help struggling readers become successful readers. Just about everyone can learn to read!

The same body of research that inspires us with optimism and hope provides the guidelines for how this can happen. While we know that many students face serious challenges to becoming skillful and motivated readers—poverty, language differences, learning difficulties, etc.—results from reading research clearly tell us that carefully designed and implemented instruction can trump these challenges. In *The Reading Coach* book (pp. 5–19), we summarized key ideas from reading research, including how to provide effective reading instruction in Chapter 2, "Foundational Knowledge for the Reading Coach."

As professional educators, we know we must teach our students to read. And, we know we *can* do it and we know *how* to do it. However, an obvious question remains: Why are so many of our students still struggling with reading? The answer has been provided by researchers who have identified a gap between the research-based "best practice" in reading instruction and the implementation of that best practice in the day-to-day world of the school classroom. Just knowing *what* should be done is only the first step in a long and sometimes difficult journey. The challenge that faces us is *how* to bridge that gap, how to help every teacher use the scientific research findings to provide effective reading instruction to every student.

Educators have attempted to address that research-to-practice gap through the process of professional development (PD). Traditionally, educators attempt to enhance and improve their teaching skills by participating in PD, which includes taking college or university coursework or online seminars, attending conferences or workshops, and reading professional literature. All of these options can and do play a valuable role in teacher PD; however, the downside is that rarely do any of these traditional forms of PD result in sustained improved practice in the classroom. Teachers often return from taking courses, participating in webinars, or attending conferences with new information and perhaps increased inspiration. They are excited, energized, and eager to try some new ideas! But then reality sets in. As teachers face the many significant daily challenges of the classroom, they too often simply return to what they already know how to do and feel comfortable doing. For anyone who has ever been a teacher, this is completely understandable. We don't need research to tell us that teaching—and change—is hard.

But then, we are right back where we started, left with wondering how to get to the point where we are truly doing our best to help every student become the best possible reader he or she can be. This is where the Reading Coach comes in.

Coaching is seen by many as an optimal form of PD because, when provided by a skillful, knowledgeable, trained, and well-supported Coach, coaching provides the missing pieces of PD: sustained, individualized, and personalized support. Effective coaching incorporates many, if not all, of the components of effective PD identified by Darling-Hammond & McLaughlin

(1996): experiential, collaborative, interactive, sustained, intensive, and connected to the teacher's day-to-day work with students as well as to a larger plan for school improvement.

Who Are Coaches?

In our work with Reading Coaches over the past several years, we've learned that the educators being asked to take on the role of Coach typically have been teaching for several years, have a strong knowledge-base in reading and literacy, and have been recognized as being skillful reading teachers. In other words, they have "walked the walk." They know and understand reading research and, importantly, how to implement research-based reading instruction that helps even highly challenged students in real-world classrooms learn to read. When Coaches have this kind of background and these credentials, they must be highly successful in providing coaching services to their colleagues, right? Well … not always. There are at least two additional components that need to be in place for Coaches to be successful.

Reading Coaches need to have training in *how* to coach! While coaching relies heavily on skills and strategies learned as a teacher, everyone who takes on this new role soon recognizes that coaching peer colleagues is very different from teaching students. One purpose of our first book for Coaches was to create a "how-to manual" that would cover some key coaching skills such as how to get started in the Coach role, how to manage time and communicate effectively, and how to use a strategic process for systematically addressing problems and engaging in Collaborative Planning. We also provided some ideas for gathering information from interviews, observations, and assessments and how to use that information to develop, support, and evaluate reading interventions. We included some ideas about designing and providing effective professional development for teachers and provided a framework for a multifaceted, systemwide approach to school improvement, which we called SAILS (Standards, Assessments, Instruction and Intervention, Leadership, Sustained Schoolwide Commitment).

Surely then, wouldn't Reading Coaches who are experienced and skillful teachers, knowledgeable about reading, and well-informed about coaching skills be successful in their work? Well … sometimes, but not always! We previously stated there were at least *two* additional components needed to be an effective Coach, and training in *how* to coach is only one of them. The other essential piece that must be in place for coaching success is *support*.

A successful Coach works within a system of support in which (1) there is sufficient *time* provided for coaching to occur; (2) the *role* of coaching has been *well-defined*; and (3) *all* key players have been fully informed about the *purpose* and the *process* of coaching, including the teachers who will work with the Coach (Bean & Zigmond, 2006). This kind of support must be provided by administration. It requires having key stakeholders at both the district and school levels (i.e., Coaches, administrators, and teachers) discuss and reach agreement about the purpose and function of a Reading Coach. These discussions and agreements should also occur at the state level if the role of Coach is supported by state-level funding.

Many of the schools, districts, and states we have worked with find that they benefit from having these kinds of discussions frequently, not just up front when the idea of providing coaching support to teachers is being initially discussed. This is due in part to the fact that the role of Reading Coach evolves and changes over time, which makes sense if you think about the essential purpose of coaching being a provision of optimal PD. As teachers receive PD support from a Coach, their need for additional PD changes; they know more, they are more effective, and they are more confident teachers. What they need from a Coach must match their new levels of skill and interest.

What Is Coaching?

If we stopped some people on the street—just average citizens—and asked them if they'd ever heard of someone who works in schools who is called a "Reading Coach," they'd likely answer "No." If we then went on to ask them to speculate about what someone called a Reading Coach might do in schools, they may suggest that perhaps these Coaches watch teachers teach reading lessons and then give the teachers feedback. Or perhaps they would hypothesize that the job of a Reading Coach is to provide guidance and support to other teachers to help them provide the best possible instruction for students. And, of course, these folks would be right! This description could definitely be recognized as a common-sense, practical view of the role of a Coach. However, as the coaching role has grown and expanded over recent years, we recognize that there are many other things that Coaches are asked to do with their time.

In fact, the number and types of tasks that Reading Coaches perform vary greatly. While the bottom-line, fundamental purpose of coaching is always related in some way to professional development, there are several different approaches to coaching that have begun to emerge in schools. We will describe four of these approaches, or models of coaching, and then explain the coaching model we developed as the basis for our work.

Four Models of Coaching

The following discussion of four different coaching models is not intended to be an exhaustive, complete, or recommended list of ways to coach. These models are simply those that we have seen being used in schools to provide coaching services.

TECHNICAL COACHING

In the technical coaching model, the primary function of the Reading Coach is to assist teachers in the accurate and high-quality implementation of a specific instructional program or strategy. Technical Coaches receive significant professional development to become experts in the materials or strategies that they will support; then, they work with colleagues to help them with issues related to successful implementation. Technical Coaches can play an important and valued role in achieving successful outcomes when professional educators use well-designed, research-supported materials with high fidelity. The Consortium for Reading Excellence (CORE) trains Coaches to use the technical coaching model.

PROBLEM-SOLVING COACHING

Problem-solving coaching involves having the Reading Coach work with one or more colleagues to address specific concerns. For a Coach, such concerns might commonly involve an academic problem (e.g., "Malique is struggling with her reading fluency") or a related behavioral issue (e.g., "Roberto isn't making the progress with his reading that I know he can make because he is off-task so often during our instructional time").

The basis for the problem-solving model of coaching comes primarily from research that was conducted in the fields of school psychology and special education. In both of these professions, practitioners are frequently called upon to collaborate with or advise colleagues about the academic, behavioral, and/or social-emotional concerns of a student. This process—typically called "consultation" in research literature—has been studied since the 1970s as a triadic, indirect service delivery model in which a *consultant* (e.g., a special educator, a school psychologist, a reading specialist) works with and through a *consultee* (often a general education teacher or a parent) to improve the outcomes of a *client* (usually a student with some kind of learning, behavioral, or emotional challenge). Sometimes, consultation can be collaborative; the consultant and the consultee pool their respective knowledge and skills to jointly attempt to solve the concern. Or, consultation can be more prescriptive; the consultant provides expert guidance to direct the resolution of the problem. For more information about the consultation process and its research base, we recommend Erchul and Sheridan (2007), Kampwirth (2006), or Sugai and Tindal (1993).

REFLECTIVE PRACTICE COACHING

When the primary function of a Reading Coach is to help teachers become more aware of their thinking about their own instructional decision-making, they are using strategies from the reflective practice model of coaching. Probably the most widely implemented version of this model is "cognitive coaching," developed by Costa and Garmston (1997). Many Coaches have received formal training in the cognitive coaching strategy, which considers the Coach a mediator who works to establish rapport with the person being coached and is viewed as a trustworthy colleague. Cognitive coaching distinguishes itself from supervision because its developers believe that only those receiving coaching can evaluate their own performance.

PEER COACHING

Peer coaching is probably the best known of all coaching models. Many acknowledge Beverly Showers and Bruce Joyce as the originators of the term "peer coaching." They started their work with coaching in the early 1980s with the hypothesis that schools could improve and students would benefit if teachers provided each other with on-site professional development.

Peer coaching started with the idea of weekly topical seminars to allow teachers to study the act of teaching. These seminars were followed up by encouraging teachers to watch each other teach and then discuss and share their ideas and reflections. In 1996, Showers and Joyce reflected about what they had learned over 15 years of studying peer coaching. One of their conclusions was that peer coaches should *not* provide verbal feedback to each other. When teachers used technical feedback techniques after an observation, Showers and Joyce documented that it was difficult to prevent coaching from slipping into something that looked and felt like supervision, and that collaborative activity among participating teachers was impaired rather than enhanced. These researchers still recommend that teachers have the opportunity to watch each other teach; however, they suggest that the debriefing after the observation should not include feedback. Rather, the observing teacher should simply comment on what she learned and how she might use what she learned in her own classroom. Showers and Joyce also suggest that a key activity of coaching should involve teachers collaboratively planning lessons and developing support materials and instructional activities.

Student-Focused Coaching (SFC) Roles

Our Student-Focused Coaching (SFC) model (Hasbrouck & Denton, 2005) is based on (1) our own work as Reading Coaches, (2) the training we have provided to Reading Coaches and administrators in university courses and inservice settings over the years, and (3) a review of the relevant research on coaching and consultation.

We define SFC as a cooperative—ideally collaborative—professional relationship, with parties mutually engaged in efforts to provide better services for students. The SFC model incorporates some of the strategies from each of the four previously described coaching models: technical, problem solving, reflective practice, and peer coaching. Depending on the needs of students and teachers, SFC Coaches function primarily in three different roles:

1. Facilitator

2. Collaborative Problem Solver

3. Teacher-Learner

FACILITATOR ROLE

While some may envision the role of a Reading Coach as being the "fixer of bad teaching," the Facilitator role for an SFC Coach takes the opposite stance. There are always teachers who are already doing a good job in their classrooms; not all teachers need to be "fixed." With those colleagues, an SFC Coach simply looks for ways to facilitate their successful efforts. A little time spent assisting with logistics (e.g., finding a missing workbook, tracking down assessment materials, helping with data entry or analysis, making a phone call to a parent) can be enormously valuable to a busy and hard-working teacher. And, because coaching is an indirect service-delivery model based on a collaborative, professional relationship, the Facilitator category also covers the time a Coach devotes to developing those relationships as well as working with administrators, supervisors, and colleagues to help define the role of the Coach.

COLLABORATIVE PROBLEM SOLVER ROLE

Because the needs of students is the primary focus, an SFC Coach collaborates with teachers to identify problems or concerns that may be preventing students from making the most reading progress possible. The Coach then leads the teacher—or a group of teachers—through a step-by-step, systematic problem-solving process that we call Collaborative Planning. The Coach and teacher(s) carefully examine the issues related to the concern, collect and analyze data to focus their efforts, develop goals, and come up with a plan of action. The plan is then implemented by the teacher, with the Coach providing support as needed. The effects of the plan are evaluated, and next steps are determined. The function of a Coach in Collaborative Planning is to manage the process effectively and efficiently, but creating the plan is a truly collaborative effort. (See Chapter 3, "Problem Solving Within SFC," for a more detailed discussion of this step-by-step process and how it can be implemented in various forms.)

TEACHER-LEARNER ROLE

The third role for SFC coaches is to provide formal, professional development to their colleagues. We use the term "Teacher-Learner" to describe this role because we have found that the outcomes of coaching are significantly enhanced by presenting and maintaining the role of Coach as a true peer of teacher colleagues. To say that Coaches will be "professionally developing" their colleagues may imply a more top-down, one-sided, expert/novice relationship that doesn't feel very equal or collaborative. Taking on the role of Coach does not confer a special tiara of power nor does it come with any kind of magic wand—as much as we may sometimes wish it did! The best and most effective Coaches know that along with effectively providing PD as needed to their colleagues, "teaching" them better ways to help them help students, they must also remain grounded in their role as learners. Coaches have a responsibility to keep themselves well-informed about the findings from high-quality, well-designed research and the resulting best-practice strategies. Subsequently, Coaches have a responsibility to help bring those ideas and strategies into full and successful implementation in their colleagues' classrooms.

Based on the research in consultation and peer coaching, we suggest that Coaches *not* engage —in any way, shape, or form—in the formal evaluation or supervision of their teacher colleagues. When they do, the research clearly suggests that the role of Coach morphs into a role that is better defined as an administrative function. This overlap can undermine the primary reason for coaching: to provide PD to teachers for best-practice instruction in classrooms.

Along with these three primary roles, we also know that Coaches—whether following the SFC model or not—are usually asked to engage in other tasks that include administration and management activities. Coaches may need to (1) attend meetings; (2) review or evaluate instructional materials; (3) communicate with others via mail, e-mail, or telephone calls; and (4) spend time completing or managing forms, paperwork, and reports. Some Coaches also may provide supervision to a paraprofessional, student teacher, or volunteer. They may need to monitor students on the playground, in bus-loading areas, hallways, or in the cafeteria. Some Coaches also teach students on a regular schedule. (We hope that Coaches also are given some time to take a lunch break or have a cup of coffee!) From time to time, every Coach may need to perform these additional tasks. We consider these to be outside the coaching role, so that any amount of time spent doing these tasks takes away from the already limited time available for actual coaching.

The Role of Administrators

We would be remiss in ending this chapter without at least quickly discussing the role of the essential partner to successful coaching: the administrator. The role of Reading Coach is so new in schools that it is being implemented in many different ways, some more successful than others. The point at which we are now, with attempts to establish the role of an onsite professional development specialist, can be rightfully compared to building an airplane while in flight. It is critical for administrators who work with Coaches to take the time to learn as much as possible about this new and exciting role.

Coaches cannot work alone; their very nature requires collaboration with peer colleagues as well as support from a supervisor. Administrator support manifests primarily in two ways: (1) assisting with the important and ongoing task of defining the role of the Reading Coach, and (2) helping Coaches find the time to do the key, essential work of coaching.

To effectively address role definition and time allocation for a Reading Coach, it is important for a school administrator to begin with a clear understanding of the fundamental purpose— the why—of coaching. As we discussed at the beginning of this chapter, the fundamental purpose is to provide sustained, individualized, and personalized professional development that bridges the gap between research and successful implementation of best practice in the classroom. Defining the role as such will help keep both the administrator and the Coach focused and effective. Helping teachers understand the role of the Reading Coach will also go a long way in minimizing the frequent fears that teachers have about a Coach being some kind of spy for the principal.

Since Coaches will rarely have all the time they need to do their job, another imperative form of support from an administrator is to minimize the amount of time that Coaches spend away from being a Facilitator, Collaborative Problem Solver, and Teacher-Learner. We have watched highly skilled and very knowledgeable Reading Coaches spend nearly all their time with administrative and managerial tasks. In these situations, these folks are not functioning as Coaches—despite their job title! They don't have sufficient time left to coach. They are functioning instead as vice principals or administrative assistants or secretaries. Clarity about the coaching role and minimizing the time spent outside of the role requires understanding and support from a Coach's key partner: the administrator.

Although we strongly believe that Coaches should not participate in the formal supervision of their peers, Coaches do need—and deserve—supervision themselves. In *The Reading Coach* book, we suggested that Coaches rarely receive adequate supervision, which we defined as specific feedback to encourage and support professional growth. Of course, one of the reasons this is not happening for many Coaches is that effective supervision requires a clear understanding of the role and the requirements of coaching. How can supervision be offered when we aren't sure of what it should look like? This is a challenge that needs to be tackled by the Coach and administrator working—and talking—together.

Summary

The role of Reading Coach can be challenging but it can also be an effective way to help provide teachers with the guidance and support they need and deserve to meet the needs of every student. The Student-Focused Coaching model was developed from an extensive research base that can help Coaches in their important work. The following chapters will provide a range of tools for Coaches to use that will make coaching a success.

Overview of Successive Chapters

In the following chapters, we will discuss

- how the SFC model works within a multitiered Response to Intervention (RTI) process (Chapter 2);
- an extension of the SFC problem-solving process (Chapter 3);
- adapting classroom reading instruction to support student growth (Chapter 4);
- using Collaborative Planning for behavior concerns (Chapter 5);
- how to effectively use classroom observations to provide coaching support to teachers (Chapter 6); and
- how to engage reluctant teachers in the coaching process (Chapter 7).

We hope you find the ideas and suggestions in this book helpful to you in your important and valuable work in helping every student become a successful reader!

2

THE ROLE OF SFC WITHIN MULTITIERED INTERVENTION APPROACHES

We know from research that students do not outgrow reading problems. In fact, students who don't learn to read in the primary grades are likely to struggle with reading throughout their school years (Francis, Shaywitz, Stuebing, Shaywitz, & Fletcher, 1996; Juel, 1988; Torgesen & Burgess, 1998) and to fall further behind in key areas like vocabulary development and general world knowledge (Stanovich, 1986). In response to this situation, many educators are suggesting that reading intervention be provided to *all* students who struggle to learn to read in the early grades. This kind of "prevention" model has the goal of "catching students before they fall" (Torgesen, 1998, p. 1).

It's clear that many students in grades 4 and above also need reading intervention; this is usually referred to as "remediation" of existing reading problems. Both prevention and remediation approaches include providing intervention to struggling readers. An intervention, strictly speaking, is an action designed to change a difficult or problematic situation. In reading instruction, intervention usually means providing some kind of specialized instruction to students who have, or who are at risk for, reading problems.

What Is "Response to Intervention" (RTI)?

The Individuals with Disabilities Education Act (IDEA) is the U.S. law that governs special education; Congress must reauthorize IDEA every few years. In its most recent iteration of this law—IDEA 2004—Congress tackled the problem of how to best identify students with learning disabilities (LD). Teachers have observed for years that many students fall through the cracks because they don't qualify as having LD, based on formulas that compare students' scores on IQ tests and achievement tests (e.g., Woodcock-Johnson® Tests of Achievement, Gates-MacGinitie Reading Tests®, Metropolitan Achievement Tests®). Researchers have found that using the difference (or "discrepancy") between these test scores is not a valid way to identify students with LD (Fletcher, Lyon, Fuchs, & Barnes, 2007).

As a result, IDEA 2004 says that school districts may use a process that includes assessment of how well students respond to quality reading intervention as part of the process of identifying students with LD. This has been called a Response to Intervention approach, or simply RTI. In an RTI approach, all students who need reading intervention receive it, and their progress is monitored through repeated assessments (e.g., measures of oral reading fluency). If a student receives high-quality intervention that most students respond well to, but still makes little progress, this can indicate a possible reading disability. The idea is to make sure a student has had a real *opportunity to learn* before we decide he/she has a disability in learning.

Implementing Schoolwide Reading Intervention

To implement the kinds of approaches we have just described, three factors must be in place in a school:

1. All students in the early grades are screened in order to identify those who may be at risk for reading difficulties.

2. Teachers provide quality classroom instruction and intervention using research-supported programs and approaches.

3. Student progress is carefully monitored to make sure that all students make enough growth in reading to meet grade-level goals.

These key ingredients of an RTI approach may sound familiar to readers of *The Reading Coach* book. The ingredients are components of the SAILS model we offered as a blueprint for supporting schoolwide reading growth. SAILS stands for **S**tandards, **A**ssessment (that's where screening and progress monitoring fit in), **I**nstruction and **I**ntervention, **L**eadership, and a **S**ustained Schoolwide Commitment with high expectations for all students. We encourage you to read or revisit *The Reading Coach* book (pp. 15–19) for more background on the SAILS model for schoolwide reading excellence.

Three-Tiered Intervention Models

Schools across the country are increasingly adopting "tiered" reading intervention models, especially in the early grades, as a way of preventing reading problems. In the most common of these models, intervention is provided at three levels. How tiered intervention models are implemented varies from state to state, and even from school to school.

In this chapter, we describe one model, but it is by no means the only tiered reading intervention approach. The key idea in all tiered models is that *all* students receive high-quality reading instruction, plus supplemental intervention if they need it. Essentially:

• In Tier 1 intervention, teachers provide high-quality classroom reading instruction to all students. If students don't make enough progress with enhanced whole-classroom instruction, they receive extra small-group reading intervention (Tier 2).

- The progress of students in Tier 2 is carefully monitored, and if they still don't show enough progress, they receive Tier 3 intervention.
- Tier 3 intervention is provided within even smaller reading groups for a longer period of time every day, often over the course of an entire school year.

We will now describe each of these tiers, although not in great detail. For a thorough description of RTI and tiered intervention approaches, see Fletcher, Denton, Fuchs, and Vaughn (2005) or Haager, Klingner, and Vaughn (2007).

TIER 1

Tier 1 intervention is quality whole-classroom reading instruction for all students. To implement Tier 1 intervention, schools typically make sure that teachers provide 60–90 minutes of uninterrupted (i.e., no announcements, assemblies, etc.) classroom reading instruction every day. But, as you know very well, it isn't enough to just "spend time" in reading instruction. For struggling readers in particular, it matters very much what teachers *do* during this instructional time. To implement Tier 1 intervention, schools adopt and use reading programs and instructional approaches that are supported by scientific reading research, and they assure that

Figure 2.1   **A Three-Tiered Reading Intervention Model**

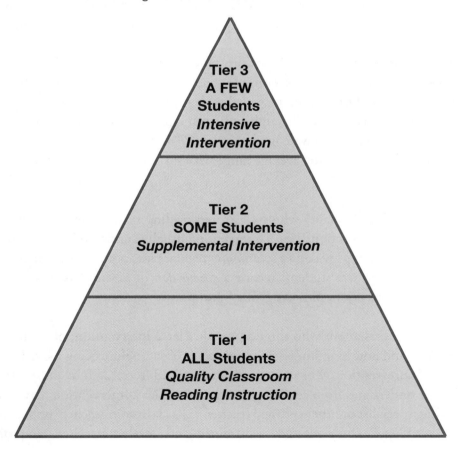

teachers have the training and support they need to implement these programs well. That's where the Reading Coach comes in! (We'll talk more about this later.)

The National Research Council concluded in their landmark report, *Preventing Reading Difficulties in Young Children* (Snow, Burns, & Griffin, 1998), that in order to learn to read English, students must

- understand and be able to apply the alphabetic principle, or how sounds are represented by print;
- practice reading enough to become fluent readers;
- learn new concepts and vocabulary; and
- learn to monitor their own reading to make sure it makes sense and to correct their mistakes if it doesn't make sense.

The report also states that it is important for teachers to provide explicit instruction in phonemic awareness and phonics, integrated with many opportunities for students to read and write meaningful connected text, both with and without teacher support and feedback. Finally, the report noted that effective teachers adapt their instruction, making changes as needed to meet the needs of each student. For example, they provide classroom reading instruction to small groups of students with similar needs. All of these are important components of enhanced Tier 1 classroom instruction. (Chapter 4 provides more information about adapting Tier 1 instruction to meet the needs of students with reading difficulties.)

Just making sure that all students receive quality classroom reading instruction can make a big difference for struggling readers. For example, Foorman, Francis, Fletcher, Schatschneider, and Mehta (1998) found that, when provided with a quality reading program that included explicit, systematic instruction in the alphabetic principle within a print-rich environment, 75% of first-grade students who were in *the bottom 20% of their classes* in reading could learn to read words (i.e., decode) in the average range without additional intervention.

TIER 2

For some students, Tier 1 quality whole-classroom reading instruction is not enough; they will need additional intervention. Tier 2 intervention usually consists of small-group (usually 3–6 students) instruction provided *in addition to* regular classroom reading instruction. It is important to note that these students receive a *double dose* of reading instruction every day: regular classroom instruction, plus extra small-group intervention.

Some controversy exists about who should provide Tier 2 intervention, how often students should receive it, and how long students should stay in Tier 2 before being moved to the more intensive Tier 3 intervention. We, and others, are involved in research to address these questions. What we understand from current research is that Tier 2 intervention may be provided by (1) a reading specialist or other certified teacher, (2) a classroom teacher (under certain circumstances), or (3) a carefully selected, well-trained, and closely supervised paraprofessional.

If a classroom teacher provides Tier 2 intervention, he or she is likely to need a good deal of support from a Reading Coach. If a paraprofessional provides the intervention, he or she will need to be trained and closely supervised by a Coach or a highly qualified, experienced master teacher. Although we don't have firm answers to the questions of the best way to schedule Tier 2 intervention, we think that students should receive this intervention for at least 20 weeks during first grade.

One option, researched by Vaughn and Linan-Thompson (2003), is to provide Tier 2 intervention every day for 30 minutes for ten weeks, then assess all students in the intervention to find out whether they have met benchmarks that indicate they will do well without further intervention. At that point, some students may exit Tier 2 intervention, but their progress should be carefully monitored to find out whether they need to go back into Tier 2 for further support. After another ten weeks of intervention, the current and previous Tier 2 students are again assessed, and the process is repeated. At that point, some students may exit intervention and others may begin or reenter Tier 2.

Vaughn and Linan-Thompson (2003) followed this process with students in the second grade, providing Tier 2 intervention to groups of three students with one teacher, outside of the regular classroom, for 30 minutes every day in addition to regular classroom reading instruction. To exit intervention, these students had to be able to read at least 50 words correctly per minute (wcpm) on grade-level text for three consecutive weeks and meet two other similar benchmarks as well. In their study, approximately 25% of the students met the benchmarks after ten weeks in Tier 2, and another 25% met the benchmarks after 20 weeks. Approximately another 25% of the students met the benchmarks after 30 weeks of intervention—the end of the school year—and the remaining 25% of students never met the benchmark. Approximately 70% of the students who left Tier 2 after ten weeks continued to make good growth in oral reading fluency for the rest of the school year without additional Tier 2 intervention.

TIER 3

In three-tiered intervention approaches, students who don't make enough progress in Tier 2 intervention are moved to Tier 3, which provides a higher level of intensity. The intensity of an intervention can be increased by (1) teaching in smaller groups, (2) increasing the length of time of intervention sessions, and (3) providing intervention over a longer period of time. Tier 3 intervention may be provided in groups of two or three students, or even one-on-one. Typically, it would be provided for close to one hour per day over the course of the entire school year, or even longer. At Tier 3, intervention would be provided by a highly trained and experienced teacher, and it would be designed to target the particular needs of each student.

You can think of Tier 3 as a kind of "intensive care" intervention for reading. Students who have already been given high-quality classroom reading instruction plus extra small-group intervention and still haven't made progress are in critical need of help. Their inability to read at grade level will have huge negative impacts—academic, social, and economic—on their lives. As in hospital intensive care units, Tier 3 reading intervention should be provided by the most experienced and effective teachers, student progress should be closely monitored (i.e., assessment every week or at least every two weeks), and instruction should be provided with high intensity. These components give struggling students the intensive reading care they need.

The Roles of the SFC Coach

The Reading Coach can be central to the success of schoolwide RTI models. The three primary roles of the SFC Coach that we described in Chapter 1—Facilitator, Collaborative Problem Solver, and Teacher-Learner—are fundamentally relevant in the application of multitiered intervention models. Also recall the three required elements for implementing a schoolwide reading intervention approach: (1) screening students to identify those with reading difficulties, (2) providing research-validated instruction along with supplemental intervention to these students, and (3) carefully monitoring student progress. The Coach supports all three of these necessary elements, within all three tiers of intervention, in all three SFC roles.

Whew! That's quite an assignment, no matter how you do the math. In the next section, we'll discuss the three coaching roles in relation to assessments—both screening and progress monitoring—and then in relation to instruction and intervention.

SFC Roles in Assessment

Reading Coaches assist in organizing and supporting teachers as they administer screening and progress-monitoring assessments. These assessments are usually brief tests of key reading and reading-related skills such as phonemic awareness, letter-sound knowledge, and oral reading fluency. Most screening and progress-monitoring measures used with elementary students require them to respond orally, and are thus administered one student at a time. In some schools, Coaches assist teachers in conducting assessments, but it is usually better if the teachers administer assessments to their own students. Teachers can learn a lot about their students' reading strengths and needs by interacting with them individually. Coaches may help cover a teacher's class for a limited amount of time while the teacher assesses individual students, but take care that this does not become an extended teaching duty. In some schools, floating substitute teachers are hired to cover classes while teachers are assessing individual students.

FACILITATOR ROLE

In general, Reading Coaches may facilitate assessment by participating in the selection of assessments, managing assessment schedules, and helping teachers manage data. Coaches may help teachers identify diagnostic assessments that can provide more detailed information for designing instruction to target students' needs. Another note of caution is in order here. We have heard from some Coaches who spend the majority of their time administering assessments and managing assessment data. Although these may be aspects of the Facilitator role, spending too much time on these jobs will limit the time the Coach can spend supporting instruction and intervention, critical elements of tiered intervention approaches. If you find yourself caught up in assessment management, we suggest that you have an open and honest talk with your supervisor about the best use of your time and skills. For more guidance, refer to the "Using Time-Management Strategies for Defining Your Role as Coach" section (pp. 31–32) in *The Reading Coach* book.

COLLABORATIVE PROBLEM SOLVER ROLE

As a problem solver, Coaches collaborate with teachers to solve assessment-related problems, and Coaches and teachers use assessment data to help define students' problems within a problem-solving process. Meeting with teachers to examine assessment results to find out why students are not making enough progress in reading can provide an excellent opportunity for a Coach to model how to use data to guide teaching decisions. This type of collaboration may provide the insight that both Coach and teacher need to solve problems and help students make accelerated growth. Collaborative problem solving becomes even more critical when students are in Tier 2 or Tier 3 intervention, since these students have already shown that they don't make enough progress with regular classroom reading instruction alone.

TEACHER-LEARNER ROLE

Besides facilitating assessment, Reading Coaches provide critical professional development (PD) in administering assessments and in interpreting and using assessment results. In training teachers to assess their students, Coaches need to stress the difference between *teaching* and *testing*. When *teaching* struggling readers, teachers provide supportive scaffolding to help students make progress. Conversely, the purpose of *testing* (assessment) is to answer questions.

Screening assessments answer the question "Which students may be at risk for reading problems and thus need more assessment and attention?" *Progress-monitoring assessments* answer the question "Is this student making enough progress in reading to reach year-end goals?" Coaches need to be sure that teachers understand that they should not help students or provide hints or reminders during student assessments. If teachers do, the assessments won't help them to accurately answer these very important questions. Teachers need to take off their "teacher" hats and put on their "tester" hats when it is time to administer assessments. (Some coaches illustrate this with actual hats during professional development.)

In general, teachers find it easier to learn how to administer assessments than how to use assessment results to make instructional decisions. It is usually helpful for a Reading Coach to provide PD and modeling in using assessment results to (1) group students for differentiated instruction, (2) plan targeted instruction to move at-risk students along, and (3) decide when to make changes in a student's instruction (e.g., provide Tier 2 intervention in addition to Tier 1 whole-classroom instruction). Co-planning lessons with teachers is a powerful tool for modeling the use of assessment data.

SFC Roles in Instruction and Intervention

In order for struggling readers to close the gap and catch up with their peers, they have to learn *faster than the average student*. Think of it as a race: if a runner is behind, he or she has to run faster to catch up. This means that students who find it difficult to learn to read have to make faster growth than students who learn more easily. This is a little mind-boggling, to say the least, but it can be done. It means that struggling readers need *more instruction* (i.e., extra Tier 2 or Tier 3 intervention) as well as *more efficient instruction* and *more opportunities for practicing* the skills they are learning.

FACILITATOR ROLE

A Reading Coach can make a valuable contribution in supporting teachers as they provide instruction to promote the accelerated progress of struggling readers. A key element of high-quality classroom reading instruction and supplemental intervention is the use of research-validated instructional approaches, curricula, and materials. Instruction can be differentiated to meet the needs of readers with varied learning needs. Coaches can help teachers select classroom reading programs and other materials based on scientific evidence of effectiveness.

A Coach can also help teachers collaborate with each other to meet the needs of all students, including those in tiered intervention. It is a well-established fact that, in schools, there is never enough time, money, or trained personnel. These realities make it challenging to provide all at-risk or struggling readers with the intervention they need. Grade-level meetings can be opportunities for teachers and administrators to share ideas and to problem-solve by thinking outside the box.

Here's an example of a determined administrator (Denton, Foorman, & Mathes, 2003): A principal of a school in which nearly all students learned to read successfully despite many challenges (e.g., neighborhood poverty, high ELL population) described the "relentless intervention" provided by the school to students who were at high risk for reading difficulties. All students in the school received 90 minutes of core classroom reading instruction every day, and classroom teachers provided additional small-group reading instruction to struggling students. If students continued to have reading difficulties, they could receive an extra 45-minute daily intervention with a reading specialist. They could also receive additional tutoring before or after school, and students who had the most severe problems received instruction from a dyslexia specialist. The principal explained, "We've built all of these safety nets to protect children who are at risk. A child who is very at risk will have a schedule that is very different from other students" (Denton et al., 2003, p. 259).

As we have alluded to, Reading Coaches may facilitate Tier 2 intervention by supervising paraprofessionals as they provide intervention to students. Research (Elbaum, Vaughn, Hughes, & Moody, 2000; Grek, Mathes, & Torgesen, 2003) has shown that non-certified paraprofessionals or preservice teachers (i.e., university students) can successfully provide Tier 2 intervention with these provisions:

1. Tutors must be carefully selected. They should
   a. have well-developed phonemic awareness (i.e., be able to segment words into sounds and blend sounds into words);
   b. be able to correctly pronounce letter-sounds;
   c. have experience working successfully with students; and
   d. demonstrate that they can learn to implement simple instructional routines.

2. The intervention approach should be clearly defined, and the curriculum should be very supportive.
   a. There should be little need for tutors to plan lessons on their own or to make key decisions about what aspects of reading to teach.
   b. Programs may be scripted, or they may be described in enough detail so that non-certified tutors can follow them easily.
   c. Programs should include a lot of hands-on active student involvement: identifying letter-sounds, reading words, sounding out words, reading text, spelling, and writing.
   d. Many effective programs include the manipulation of letter or word cards, magnetic letters, or other tools, increasing active involvement.

3. Intervention group sizes should be kept small to make behavior management easier. We suggest groups of three (or fewer) students.

4. Tutors should receive sufficient training and ongoing coaching support so that they can implement the intervention with high fidelity, maintain positive relationships with students, and keep students on-task and actively involved.

A cautionary note to the Coach: Selecting, training, supervising, and coaching a group of tutors can be a full-time job. A school will probably need more than one Reading Coach if this is to be part of your assignment.

COLLABORATIVE PROBLEM SOLVER ROLE

Since the point of a schoolwide intervention model is to accelerate the progress of struggling readers, there are many opportunities for systematic problem solving within all three tiers of intervention. Problem solving has a uniquely important role in Tiers 2 and 3, since students at these levels have already failed to make progress in Tier 1. It can be very helpful to have a Coach observe an intervention lesson, with a focus on how the student is reacting to the instruction. Sometimes, intervention teachers know they need to make changes in instruction but have a hard time figuring out exactly what needs to be changed. This is the perfect opportunity for a Coach and teacher to use the collaborative problem-solving process in the SFC model.

TEACHER-LEARNER ROLE

Professional development is key to improving the quality of reading instruction and intervention. As teacher-learners, SFC Coaches provide PD to individual teachers or groups of teachers. PD may include workshops on topics such as implementing adopted research-based reading programs, adopting instructional strategies and routines shown by research to be most effective for students with reading difficulties, and other related topics. Modeling, co-planning lessons, observing instruction, and discussing student reactions to instruction are important ways in which Coaches support the implementation of tiered reading intervention. (See Chapter 6 in this book for an observation routine that includes all of these coaching activities.) As discussed in Chapter 8 of *The Reading Coach* book, PD should be planned carefully based on the needs of students and teachers, and it should be a unified

Table 2.1 **Possible Roles of the SFC Reading Coach in a Schoolwide Intervention Model**

	Facilitator	Collaborative Problem-Solver	Teacher-Learner
Assessment (screening and progress monitoring)	• Cover classes so that teachers can administer assessments to their own students. • Help select assessments. • Help manage assessment schedules. • Help teachers manage data.	• Work with teachers to solve assessment-related problems. • Use data to help define reading problems in the Collaborative Planning process.[a]	• Provide PD in administering assessments and using assessment data. • Model the use of data to inform instruction by co-planning lessons with teachers.
Instruction and Intervention (Tier 1, Tier 2, and Tier 3)	• Help select research-validated instructional materials. • Facilitate collaboration among teachers in meeting the needs of all students. • Supervise paraprofessionals who provide Tier 2 intervention. • Help administrators obtain and schedule PD in new core classroom-reading programs.	• Engage in Collaborative Planning with teachers to promote accelerated progress of Tier 2 and Tier 3 students.[a] • Problem-solve with teachers and administrators when obstacles arise in implementing the schoolwide intervention approach.	• Provide PD in the use of new instructional approaches. • Provide PD in adapting classroom instruction for students with learning difficulties.[b] • Observe and model effective instruction.[c] • Co-plan lessons with teachers. • Model self-reflection about instruction.[c]

[a] See Chapter 3.
[b] See Chapter 4.
[c] See Chapter 6.

and coordinated effort with specific objectives, not a series of disconnected meetings and workshops.

Summary

These are exciting times for those who work with struggling readers:

- Researchers have learned a great deal about what it takes to teach almost all students to read.

- Federal and state governments are recognizing that many students need reading intervention and that professional educators shouldn't wait for students to fail before providing them with specialized instruction.

- IDEA 2004 states that a percentage of special-education funding may be used to provide intervention in schoolwide models like those we have described in this chapter.

If approaches and materials validated through reading research are going to be implemented in schools, teachers will need support. *Table 2.1* illustrates some roles of the Reading Coach in schoolwide tiered reading intervention models.

We believe that the Reading Coach—acting as a facilitator, problem solver, and teacher-learner—can make a difference in whether these initiatives succeed in changing the lives as well as the academic, social, and economic futures of struggling students. We must not miss this golden opportunity to make a difference!

3

PROBLEM SOLVING WITHIN SFC

Reading Coaches who use the SFC model engage in tasks in three different categories: Facilitator, Collaborative Problem Solver, and Teacher-Learner. We find that SFC Coaches seem to spend a significant amount of time in the role of Collaborative Problem Solver, using our systematic problem-solving strategy to engage in Collaborative Planning with their colleagues. Coaches find that using the step-by-step process with a teacher helps to

- keep the focus of coaching where it should be—on students;

- build a sense of partnership and shared purpose with the teacher's peers; and

- develop good plans for taking the next step to help each student succeed.

In this chapter, we
- review key "big ideas" from *The Reading Coach* book about the rationale and processes of Collaborative Planning;
- discuss a less formal problem-solving process; and
- describe a team problem-solving approach.

Comparing Three Coaching Approaches

The foundational purpose of coaching is professional development (PD): assisting teachers to effectively implement research-based, best-practice strategies to help every student succeed. There are three different ways that Reading Coaches can go about providing PD to their colleagues.

DIRECTIVE APPROACH

One way a Coach can provide PD to teachers is to use a *directive approach*: a Coach watches a colleague teach a lesson for the purpose of making evaluative decisions about the quality of the instruction, and then follows up with specific feedback about what aspects of the lesson were performed effectively and what aspects can be modified or otherwise improved. The Coach might offer to model or demonstrate how the lesson should be taught or make suggestions to the teacher about how to improve the lesson design or delivery. The obvious drawback to this method of coaching is that most teachers don't enjoy having a peer colleague (or anyone, for that matter) watch them teach and then give them corrective feedback. Coaches who take this approach may find it difficult to be invited back to a teacher's classroom for a second visit.

"EXPERT" APPROACH

Another way for Reading Coaches to offer PD to their colleagues is to provide solutions to each and every concern a teacher might have. When teachers need help and ask a Coach for assistance, certainly the Coach can offer a possible solution. However, the pitfalls inherent in this method of coaching should be considered:

- Coaches who set themselves up to be the "all-knowing experts" may (consciously or unconsciously) place themselves on a pedestal. When this happens, teachers tend to view the Coach as unapproachable, not as a peer colleague with a shared interest in helping students succeed—a strong position from which to offer support. Certainly better than from the top of a shaky pedestal!

- When a Coach offers a best-guess solution to a teacher for every problem, there will likely come a time when a teacher's problem is *not* one for which the Coach has an appropriate resolution. When that time comes, teachers may begin to perceive the Coach as a failure or as being unhelpful.

A COLLABORATIVE PROBLEM-SOLVING APPROACH

While the previous two approaches to coaching may be just what some teachers want, from our own experiences as Reading Coaches—as well as the results of research studies on coaching and related systems—we long ago concluded that neither of these alternatives is the most effective way to coach. As an option, we developed the SFC model of coaching, in which the Coach works as a side-by-side peer partner, linking arms in collaboration and together maintaining a shared focus on the needs of every student.

However, in reality, many Coaches struggle with at least one or two colleagues who are less-than-thrilled with the idea of collaboration. A common concern voiced among Coaches is: "How can I convince the more reluctant teachers to work with me?" Does that sound somewhat familiar? We've found that one of the very best ways to create a cooperative partnership with even reluctant teachers is to use the Systematic Problem Solving (SPS) strategy for Collaborative Planning. SPS helps keep Coaches from feeling as if they somehow have to be the "teaching police" or the magical source for all possible answers. Collaborative Planning—using a systematic problem-solving strategy—is powerful for two reasons:

1. Investing time in Collaborative Planning is an effective way to lay a foundation for a trusting, respectful, professional relationship between Coach and teacher colleague. A Coach understands that his or her role *relies* on the existence of this kind of relationship, so investing time in a process that can lead to this outcome can be a very wise choice.

2. Collaborative Planning can be used to develop realistic, effective plans that have at least a reasonable chance of helping to resolve any number of concerns.

An Overview of the Systematic Problem-Solving Strategy

Our systematic problem-solving strategy is typically used in 1:1 coaching situations with a Reading Coach and a single teacher, often with a focus on an academic concern about a single student. There are variations on the basic structure, however. The strategy can be adapted for use with a team of colleagues, to address a concern about a group of students or an entire classroom, or to address behavioral or emotional concerns. We will discuss some of these variations later in this chapter.

We developed the problem-solving process used by SFC Coaches by reviewing the research on problem solving. That review let us know that many different professions have developed specific strategies to address problems or concerns that arise within their own, unique area of professional focus. However, it was also clear that all of the strategies seemed to have four common phases or stages. Every process involves

- figuring out what the problem is;
- developing a plan of action to address the identified problem;
- implementing the plan; and
- eventually evaluating the results of the implementation and taking any necessary follow-up steps.

We used these generic components to develop a four-phase problem-solving strategy designed specifically for use in SFC for Collaborative Planning.

As Reading Coaches begin the collaborative-planning process, one thing to keep in mind is that the plan that will ultimately be developed through mutual efforts and has a chance of working only if it is actually implemented. The best plan in the world won't work if it isn't used. Usually, the person who is going to implement the plan is the teacher, *not* the Coach. A common error that Coaches make is to guide the problem-solving process in a direction that makes *them* feel comfortable. Novice Coaches tend to push for a plan that feels right to them, that they could implement, that they believe will be successful. The research on problem solving makes it clear that there are some key considerations that need to be in place to increase the likelihood that a teacher will ultimately use the plan successfully in his or her classroom:

1. The teacher must believe that the plan will be effective.
2. The plan should not require a lot of time or materials to implement.
3. The plan must match the teacher's philosophies and beliefs.
4. The plan should be minimally intrusive to existing classroom routines.
5. The teacher needs to have a sense of control over the implementation.

Coaches need to be sure that the teacher feels ownership of the process throughout all four phases. Keeping all participants as equally involved as possible at every step contributes to the sense of collaboration. Remember, the plan is for use by the *teacher*; it is not the Coach's plan.

The Roles of the Reading Coach and the Teacher in Collaborative Planning

What is the role of the Reading Coach in Collaborative Planning? It is definitely *not* a Coach's job to come up with the perfect plan that is sure to solve the problem. But, a Coach does have a specific responsibility in Collaborative Planning: to manage the collaborative work *effectively* and *efficiently*. Collaborative Planning can be managed *effectively* when a Coach

- thoroughly understands the purpose of the process;
- knows the steps involved in each phase of the process;
- helps keep the focus on each step; and
- completes the steps in the right order.

To manage Collaborative Planning *efficiently*, a Coach needs to move as quickly as possible through all four phases of the strategy.

The speed with which a process can be completed depends on two aspects that are directly related to the dual purpose of Collaborative Planning—solving the problem and building a collaborative relationship. If a student's concern is complex and the Coach and teacher have not worked together before on a collaborative plan, the Coach will likely want to move more slowly and deliberately through the four phases of specific problem solving. If, on the other hand, the problem is rather straightforward and the teacher and Coach already know, trust, and respect each other, Collaborative Planning can progress quickly.

While the Coach alone takes responsibility for managing the process, both participants have equal responsibility to work together to develop, effectively implement, and evaluate the outcomes of a plan that is based on data, reflects best practice strategies, and is responsive to the teacher's needs, resources, and skills. To accomplish this, it is important for the teacher to enter the process knowing what is going to occur. This is especially important if the Coach has previously been using either of the less effective models of coaching: the more directive method or the expert answer provider. Coaches must take time to explain how Collaborative Planning works before they can effectively use it together. They may also need to explain why they will now be less eager to offer "on-the-spot" solutions to their colleagues' concerns.

The Four Phases of Collaborative Planning

PHASE 1: PROBLEM PRESENTATION

In the first phase of Collaborative Planning, the Reading Coach makes initial contact with a teacher to hear about his or her concern. A Coach should remember the *dual* purpose of the process at all times—to solve the problem and to build or solidify a collaborative relationship with the teacher. Phase 1 presents a wonderful opportunity to focus on both of these goals. It is important for the Coach to begin by getting a sense of the teacher's perspective on the problem and to hear details such as how long the problem has been occurring and what the teacher has already tried to resolve the problem. Coaches need to listen with a sympathetic ear and to respond with empathy and understanding, while at the same time maintaining an objective stance, thinking about what might be contributing to or causing the problem.

Once the teacher presents an overview of the problem, the next step is to determine what data might be needed to get as accurate a picture of the concern as possible. This step may include collecting data from observations, assessments, interviews, or record reviews. (We describe in detail the strategies a Coach can use to collect this kind of data for problem solving in Chapter 6 of *The Reading Coach* book). To the extent possible, data collection should be divided between the Coach and the teacher to underscore the collaborative nature of this process. Set a reasonable date for the next meeting, allowing enough time to complete the data-collection plan. Phase 1 meetings should typically take 15–30 minutes.

PHASE 2: DEFINE THE PROBLEM, SET GOALS, DEVELOP A PLAN

This is a key phase of Collaborative Planning and a lot needs to happen here. As you will see, Phase 2 work can take a significant amount of time. Sometimes, this phase will need to happen over a couple of meetings rather than in just one.

Define the Problem

The Phase 2 meeting should begin with a collaborative sharing and analysis of all the data collected between Phase 1 and Phase 2. After examining the data, both the Reading Coach and the teacher may decide that more information is needed before moving forward. If so, decide what additional data to collect, who is going to collect it, and by what date. Then, set a date and time for another Phase 2 meeting.

If both the Coach and the teacher agree that they have enough information to proceed, the next step in the process is for them to collaboratively define the problem. A short summary —perhaps one to three sentences—will create a shared focus for collaborative efforts. A problem definition should be written down if the targeted problem is complex. If not, a verbal summary that both the Coach and the teacher agree is accurate is usually sufficient. Sometimes—too often, it seems—students who need assistance have needs in multiple areas: academic, behavioral, or even social/emotional. So, part of the work in developing a problem definition may include prioritizing what problem(s) to address first. If we don't prioritize, it is nearly impossible to create a plan of action. No plan can take care of every concern when the problems are numerous or complex. A prioritized list also helps to ensure that we won't forget about the other, perhaps less critical, concerns. After taking care of the higher-priority concerns, the Coach and the teacher may revisit this list and develop another plan in the future.

Set Goals

As anxious as everyone is at this point to get going on a solution, there are still a couple of other very important steps to take. The first is to set some goals. This part of Collaborative Planning can be fun because it involves a big shift in the conversation. Up until this point, the focus has been the *problem*—what the student can't do, won't do, always does inappropriately, etc. Now we get to dream about the future! What will this student do differently if the plan we are going to develop works the way we hope? Reading Coaches may need to work with a teacher to set a reasonable number of goals—typically, one to three—that are sufficiently concrete. Well-defined goals that can be objectively measured will be needed eventually to evaluate whether or not the plan has been effective.

Some teachers haven't had much experience with setting specific goals and may need a bit of assistance with this step. During this step, a teacher may say something like:

> "My goal for Edward is that he just do what's right instead of what's wrong all the time. I know he knows the difference."

The Coach might respond by saying:

> "You know, that's a great goal for Edward. We absolutely do need to come up with a plan to help him make the right choices with his behavior. But we will also eventually need to have a way to measure or track his progress. What specifically do we want to see him doing or not doing in the future?"

Goals made within the Collaborative Planning process can be both *overt* (public, discussed openly by the teacher and Coach) and *covert* (private, or developed by the Coach only). The Coach who is working with Edward's teacher may have concluded that one of the reasons that Edward's behavior is not acceptable is that the teacher does not appear to have sufficient knowledge about how to set up a classroom management system and does not effectively use positive reinforcement with her students. In such a case, the Coach may set up one or more covert goals, or goals that the Coach will be working on that are not shared with the teacher. In this case, the Coach might set covert goals of having Edward's teacher set up and effectively manage her classroom and to significantly increase the number of positive comments she makes to her students. If the Coach has gathered data on these concerns, she may also be able to establish concrete covert goals.

Develop a Plan

One final step remains before an action plan is developed. The Coach and teacher need to decide how the overt goals they collaboratively established will be evaluated. If the goals are sufficiently concrete, the evaluation plan will be easy. For example:

> Edward will decrease his off-task behaviors (sleeping in class, being out of his seat without permission, talking to other students, etc.) from 74% to 40% in 3 weeks.

Once the evaluation plan for the overt goals has been developed and clarified, it is time to develop a plan of action. The Coach may want to start this step by saying:

> "We've done a lot of work together over the past couple of weeks to figure out what's going on with Edward. We decided what behaviors to focus on, and we've set some

exciting goals for Edward. Now, we have to figure out a plan for helping Edward reach those goals. Do you have any ideas about what you might want to try?"

If a teacher does not have any—or perhaps only one or two—ideas, the Coach can respond by offering suggestions for consideration. Rather than trying to come up with the plan single-handedly, it is best for the Coach to create a menu of options from which the teacher can choose. Remember: Keeping all participants as equally involved as possible at every step contributes to the sense of collaboration, which is one purpose for the whole SPS process. Using Collaborative Planning is just one way that Coaches offer professional development to colleagues. Some teachers will need only a bit of coaching support (the Facilitator role of SFC), while others may need a great deal of assistance from the Coach (the Teacher-Learner role of SFC). Either way, keep the focus on helping the student, and deepen the collaborative partnership with a colleague. That is coaching at its best!

Inherent in Phase 2 is determining *when* to evaluate the student's progress toward reaching the established goals. The Coach and the teacher need to make a reasonable best-guess estimate of how long it might take for their action plan to show some effect. It is possible that different goals will be evaluated at different times, because some goals may be quickly reached while others may take some time to accomplish. Together, the Coach and the teacher determine a time to hold a *Phase 4 Evaluation* meeting (description follows).

The last step of Phase 2 is for the Coach and the teacher to have a conversation about how the Coach can provide support to the teacher while the plan is being implemented. Common questions in this conversation include:

- Does the Coach need to come to the classroom to model some of the techniques or strategies that will be used in the plan?
- Are there forms that need to be developed for student self-monitoring or recordkeeping?
- Does someone need to inform the student's parents or other teachers about the plan?
- Who is going to discuss the plan with the student?
- Can the Coach periodically stop by the classroom to check how things are going?
- Are there other ways a Coach can offer support to the teacher?

Phase 2 is then wrapped up by the Coach, who summarizes all the important work that has been accomplished: defining the problem, clarifying and setting goals, developing the action plan, and identifying how the Coach can support the teacher during Phase 3.

PHASE 3: IMPLEMENT THE PLAN
In this phase of Collaborative Planning, the teacher implements the plan that was collaboratively developed by the Reading Coach and the teacher, with the Coach providing support. Phase 3 can occur over a period of a couple of days, a few weeks, or even a few months,

depending on the plan that is being implemented. Over this period of time, it is not uncommon for the plan to need a bit of adjusting. Once the teacher gets back to the day-to-day reality of her classroom, unanticipated challenges often arise that must be addressed. It is critical for the Coach to be available to provide support and guidance, especially in the very early stages of Phase 3. If a teacher is left alone and the inevitable problems, issues, or confusions arise, it is not uncommon for the teacher to simply drop the plan and then end up feeling as if all the time spent in the first two phases was wasted. We certainly do not want that to happen!

PHASE 4: EVALUATION AND NEXT STEPS

During Phase 2, the Reading Coach and the teacher estimated a timeline for when to evaluate the effectiveness of the plan. That original timeline may be modified to move the evaluation up if things are going well or push it back a bit if the plan obviously needs more time to work. The decisions in this Phase 2 meeting will determine the next steps to take for each overt goal.

1. *If the goal was achieved:*
   - Do we end the plan immediately or phase out the plan over time?
   - Do we want to go back to the problem definition in Phase 2, look at other needs, and begin the process of developing a new goal or two and then a new plan to address the new goals?

2. *If the goal was not achieved:*
   - Do we want to adjust the goal?
   - Do we want to eliminate the goal?
   - Do we want to make changes in the plan?
   - Do we want to let the plan run a bit longer? (The student might not have achieved the goal, but he/she made some progress.)

A similar—but private—process will be done solely by the Coach to assess covert goals the Coach set for the teacher in terms of changes in skills, strategies, attitudes, beliefs, etc.

Collaborative Planning: The Quick Version

Using the four-phase systematic problem-solving process for Collaborative Planning with a colleague is a very powerful tool for Reading Coaches. The time invested can reap valuable rewards: effectively helping a student struggling with academic or behavioral issues *plus* an improved professional relationship with a colleague.

However, as you can see by reading through the overview, Collaborative Planning can take a significant amount of time; and sometimes, we simply need to move a bit faster. If the concern is relatively simple, if relevant information or data is readily available, and if the teacher and Coach have already established a collaborative relationship, the process can move very quickly. Here's an example of quick Collaborative Planning from a personal experience of a Reading Coach:

> (Some background: This is a teacher with a very different philosophy and style of teaching than the Coach. However, the Coach learned by working with this teacher in different capacities that her methods work. Her students are thriving, are learning, and are managing their behaviors well in an environment that is positive, accepting, and encouraging for every student—despite the seeming chaos and a rather *laissez-faire* classroom management system. These two educators—initially quite wary and even judgmental of each other—over time developed a collaborative, trusting, and respectful professional relationship.)
>
> The teacher approaches the Coach in the hallway and asks the Coach to look at a paper in her hand—a partially completed worksheet, with very sloppy writing and many errors. The teacher says, "I've tried everything I know to do for Shelly, but she still takes *forever* to do her written work, and you can see she's still hasn't gotten it yet. I'm getting so frustrated! Do you have any suggestions?"
>
> The Coach first asks the teacher to tell her what she has already tried with Shelly. After listening to the teacher's answers, the Coach makes a suggestion. The teacher says, "Hmmm ... OK, I'll try it," and heads back to her classroom.
>
> A week or so goes by. The next time the Coach sees this teacher is in the staff room, having a cup of coffee and grading papers. The teacher looks up and calls the Coach over to her table.
>
> "Hey, I want to show you something," she says, as she pulls out a couple of papers from the pile in front of her. "Look how well Shelly did on these papers. I tried your suggestion and it worked great. Thanks!"

This story may seem to have nothing to do with the Collaborative Planning process but, in fact, is a wonderful example of a condensed version of Collaborative Planning:

Phase 1: The teacher and Coach meet in a hallway. The teacher informs the Coach what she believes the problem to be. Because the teacher has data (Shelly's initial paper) with her—and that data is sufficient to identify the target problem—they move directly to Phase 2.

Phase 2: There is no need to develop a problem definition or articulate a goal because both the problem itself and the teacher's goal are quite clear: Shelly needs to complete her written assignments accurately and in a reasonable amount of time. In this case, the action plan is developed completely by the Coach, as the teacher had already tried everything she knew. There was also no need to develop a support plan; the Coach believed the teacher could implement the suggestion by herself. (In this scenario, Phase 1 *and* Phase 2 took about 4 minutes total.)

Phase 3: The teacher used the Coach's suggestion with Shelly.

Phase 4: The teacher and the Coach met in the faculty room. Two of Shelly's successfully completed papers provided evidence to use in an evaluation. The suggested plan worked! (Phase 4 took about 1 minute.)

As you can see, all of the essential problem-solving elements are there, but they occurred over a brief period of time. That was completely appropriate in this situation for the following reasons:

- The problem was minor and narrowly focused.

- The teacher already had data (i.e., Shelly's paper) for the Coach, which allowed the process to move from a "presenting" problem to a targeted, defined problem (no need for additional data collection between Phases 1 and 2).

- Very importantly, the Coach and this teacher already had an established, collaborative, professional relationship. The Coach knew that, in this case, offering an on-the-spot suggestion would not cause this teacher to perceive the Coach as someone up on a pedestal, *the* person with *all* the right answers. The Coach also knew that the suggestion she made was something the teacher was capable of carrying out herself (i.e., the teacher had the necessary skills and strategies to carry out the suggestion), so no Phase 3 support was required.

We offer this example to make sure that Coaches understand that Collaborative Planning is an effective tool that can be used flexibly in different ways for different needs and situations—from simple and straightforward to complex and multifaceted.

Team Problem Solving

Another way for a Coach to use a strategic problem-solving strategy is with a team of teachers and specialists, rather than with a single teacher. Many schools have Student Study Teams or Student Support Teams or Schoolwide Assistance Teams for group problem solving. However, not all of these types of teams are considered to be very effective or efficient; in fact, we sometimes find that team meetings eat up a lot of time but in the end do not accomplish much. But, we keep trying. Why is that?

Well, we pull together teams of busy professional educators for problem-solving meetings because we simply need as many *brains* at the table as possible to deal with the complex problems we face in schools. One downside of this—and the reason many team meetings are not successful—is that all those brains come with *mouths*. When we get a group of smart, passionate, resourceful professionals together at one time, there are going to be a lot of ideas and opinions to share, and that simply takes a lot of time. Another potential downside is a tendency for one (or more) individual to dominate, or even completely take over, the process and cut out other team members. This leaves folks justifiably wondering why they have taken precious time away from their own work to sit and listen to the same individuals giving their opinions over and over again.

So, do we just give up on trying to solve problems using a team approach? No—we look for a better way to deal with the inherent challenges of working with a team: spending too much time not accomplishing much.

Our recommendation is to use a time-structured problem-solving system. Many years ago, we learned about an efficient 25-minute team problem-solving strategy developed by colleagues Randy Sprick, Marilyn Sprick, and Mickey Garrison. They originally described this system in *Interventions: Collaborative Planning for Students at Risk* (Sprick, Sprick, & Garrison, 1993), and it is included in a new book, *B-RTI: Behavioral response to intervention: Creating a continuum of problem-solving and support* (Sprick, Booher, & Garrison, 2009). Over the years, we have shared this method with Reading Coaches across the country and have heard glowing reports about how—finally—their team meetings were running efficiently and that functional plans were being developed. We would like to share two separate versions of this problem-solving strategy with you: one to address student behavior concerns and another to address student academic concerns. While the steps of each strategy vary somewhat, there are two identical tasks that must be completed before holding a team problem-solving meeting: forming the team and assigning roles to three team members.

WHO SERVES ON THE TEAM?

The makeup of the team is flexible; every school will have different key people who should serve on a problem-solving team. Some schools have found it helpful to have the subject student's parents attend these meetings, while others do not include parents on a regular basis. (Please note that if parents are invited to attend these meetings, it is important for a team member to carefully explain the process to them *before the meeting*. Otherwise, parents may feel as if they are being rushed or that their child is being short-changed.)

Some schools find that rotating team members is a good idea, perhaps making serving on the problem-solving team a shared duty along with supervising hallways or working on the school social committee. Along with rotating members, there may be some individuals who attend every meeting. Depending on your staff, these regular members might include the school counselor, social worker, school psychologist, nurse, reading specialist, or Reading Coach.

As valuable as it might be to have many of these specialists at the table for each meeting, another consideration is the size of the team. Teams with four or fewer members seem a bit small, and teams with ten or more members often feel too big. We typically suggest that a team with between five and eight members is probably just about right.

ASSIGNING ROLES: LEADER, TIMEKEEPER, RECORDER

One of the keys to making this 25-minute strategy work well is to assign the roles of Leader, Timekeeper, and Recorder to three team members. These roles should be rotated on a timetable of the team's choosing. If the problem-solving team is meeting to address the concerns of a single teacher, that teacher should not assume any of these roles.

The job of the Leader is to effectively manage the problem-solving process. The Leader is *not* in charge of the development of the plan nor does the Leader get to speak more than other team members. The Leader's primary responsibilities are to make sure that

- each person on the team has an equal opportunity to participate in each step of the problem-solving process (i.e., prevents any one person from dominating the process);
- the team stays focused on doing the work of each step—not jumping ahead or skipping over a step; and
- the guidelines for the amount of time allocated for each step are followed.

The team problem-solving strategy will break down if the Leader does not stick to recommended time guidelines for each step in the problem-solving process. Of course, there will be occasions when the team is making great strides on a step, but time simply runs out. In that case, the Leader may make a recommendation to the group to consider extending the time a bit (e.g., "We aren't quite done with our work on this step. Would everyone agree to extend this step by two minutes?"). Also, the opposite sometimes happens, when the group wraps up all the work they need to accomplish on a step before time runs out. In that case, the Leader would check with the group to determine if there is agreement on moving on to the next step. There is no provision for "banking" unused minutes (or seconds) from one step to another; that would ultimately become too confusing.

While the basic structure of this process is designed for a 25-minute meeting, there are alternative timelines for a 35-minute or 50-minute team meeting (see *Tables 3.1* and *3.2*, following). Some teams find it helpful to use the 35-minute structure for their first few meetings. Once team members are comfortable with the process, they may want to continue to allocate 35 minutes for future meetings, spending the first 10 minutes reviewing evaluation data from previous problem-solving meetings and then subsequently using the 25-minute timeline for the meeting itself.

The Timekeeper's job is to keep track of the time allocated for each step in the problem-solving strategy and to let the Leader know when about 30 seconds remain in the current step. The Recorder keeps notes, writing down key decisions at each step. The Recorder should not feel as if he or she needs to become an official courtroom stenographer, writing down everything that is said. Typically, at the conclusion of the meeting, the notes are handed to the teacher who sought assistance from the team. Teachers are best served with short and succinct notes: the key ideas and a copy of the problem-solving plan developed by the team.

Aside from completing these assigned tasks, the team members who take on the roles of Leader, Timekeeper, and Recorder are expected to fully participate in the problem-solving process as all other meeting participants. Sprick, Sprick, and Garrison (1993) recommend that these roles be assigned to different people from meeting to meeting. For example, the Reading Coach should not always be the meeting Leader because that might imply that the Coach has some additional power or authority that does not come with that position.

Little formal training is needed to make this problem-solving process successful, but everyone who is going to participate should know ahead of time about a few basic compliance rules:

1. Participants should have learned about the steps of the process before the first meeting. (We have provided a one-page form for both the behavior problem-solving process and the academic problem-solving process in the *Appendix*. It is most helpful for every team member to have a copy of the appropriate form during a meeting.)

2. Team members must agree to stick to the topic and purpose of each step.

3. Everyone needs to follow the time guidelines, with only minor adjustments to extend a step or to move on if the work on the current step is finished.

4. Team members should fully participate in the problem-solving process so that all the good ideas proposed at the table are shared.

Many schools and districts have developed policies regarding the use of problem-solving teams, which may include a requirement to notify parents or even obtain parental permission before a meeting can be held to specifically discuss an individual student. Be sure that you are aware of any such policies and that you are following all the relevant requirements and procedures.

Team Problem Solving: Student Behavior Concerns

Note: Chapter 5, "Collaborative Planning for Student Behavior Concerns," provides information on how to develop and implement effective intervention plans for student behavior concerns. It may be beneficial for the Coach to read through that chapter—or even conduct professional development training for teachers on the chapter's content—before participating in a 25-minute team meeting for student behavior concerns.

PRIOR TO MEETING
Contact parent(s) or guardian(s) as school policy or the situation requires.

STEP 1: COLLECT BACKGROUND INFORMATION
This step begins with the teacher:

- describing the concern about the student;
- providing as much detail as possible about the problem behavior (e.g., when, where, how often, for how long);
- describing the student's strengths; and
- identifying the strategies that he or she has already tried to effect change.

Team members may ask questions to get a better sense of the situation; however, *no solutions may be offered at this early step*. Also, leading questions or comments that imply what the

Table 3.1   **Recommended Timelines for Team Problem Solving (Behavior)**

STRUCTURED INTERVENTION PLANNING for BEHAVIOR CONCERNS	25-minute meeting	35-minute meeting	50-minute meeting
Step 1 COLLECT BACKGROUND INFORMATION	6 min.	7 min.	10 min.
Step 2 IDENTIFY THE PROBLEM AND SET GOALS	2 min.	3 min.	4 min.
Step 3 DETERMINE CORRECTIVE CONSEQUENCES	2 min.	3 min.	4 min.
Step 4 SPECIFY RESPONSIBLE AND IRRESPONSIBLE BEHAVIORS	4 min.	6 min.	8 min.
Step 5 BRAINSTORM PROACTIVE STRATEGIES	4 min.	6 min.	8 min.
Step 6 CREATE THE PLAN	3 min.	4 min.	8 min.
Step 7 FINAL DETAILS: EVALUATION AND SUPPORT	4 min.	6 min.	8 min.

Adapted from *B-RTI: Behavioral response to intervention: Creating a continuum of problem-solving and support* (Sprick, Booher, & Garrison, 2009)

teacher *should* have done must be avoided (e.g., "Didn't you use positive reinforcement with this kid?"; "It sounds like you didn't establish a very positive relationship with this student."). The team's function is to help and support—not criticize or embarrass—a colleague.

STEP 2: IDENTIFY THE PROBLEM AND SET GOALS

The team works with the teacher to narrow the scope of the problem, if necessary, and to identify one to three goals.

STEP 3: DETERMINE CORRECTIVE CONSEQUENCES

The team determines whether irresponsible or inappropriate behavior will be corrected, ignored, or whether a consequence will be implemented by the teacher.

STEP 4: SPECIFY RESPONSIBLE AND IRRESPONSIBLE BEHAVIORS

The team specifies concrete examples of responsible behaviors and/or student strengths to encourage as well as examples of irresponsible behaviors to discourage. This step is essential because the teacher who works with the student will need to be very clear about what he or she wants the student to do and not do. The teacher *must* be consistent in the administration of any consequences or reinforcement.

STEP 5: BRAINSTORM PROACTIVE STRATEGIES

The team brainstorms ideas for how to encourage the student to increase responsible personal behaviors. The Leader should elicit as many ideas as possible from all meeting attendees. Avoid discussing, criticizing, or dismissing ideas as they come up—or promoting your own ideas as being the best.

STEP 6: CREATE THE PLAN

The teacher presenting the student behavior problem selects a manageable number of proactive strategies suggested in Step 5 to implement. Generally, it is best if other team members *do not talk* during this step, except to answer any questions the teacher may have about any of the strategies. The problem-solving plan has to be created by the teacher(s) because it will be used in his or her own classroom.

STEP 7: FINAL DETAILS: EVALUATION AND SUPPORT

The team

- helps develop at least two ways to determine the plan's effectiveness in achieving the goal(s) identified in Step 2;
- identifies what other adults can do to assist the student and the teacher (be specific—who, what, when, where); and
- identifies who will discuss the plan with the student and when this discussion will take place.

The meeting ends with the scheduling of a follow-up meeting to track the effectiveness of the plan. At that follow-up meeting, the same questions raised in Phase 4 of the SPS process will need to be addressed:

1. *If the goal was achieved:*
   - Do we end the plan immediately or phase out the plan over time?
   - Do we want to go back to the problem definition in Step 2, look at other needs, and begin the process of developing a new goal or two and then a new plan to address the new goals?

2. *If the goal was not achieved:*
   - Do we want to adjust the goal?
   - Do we want to eliminate the goal?
   - Do we want to make changes in the plan?
   - Do we want to let the plan run a bit longer? (The student might not have achieved the goal, but he/she made some progress.)

Team Problem Solving: Student Academic Concerns

Note: Chapter 2 and Chapter 7 in *The Reading Coach* book provide information on how to develop and implement effective intervention plans for student academic concerns. It may be

Table 3.2 **Recommended Timelines for Team Problem Solving (Academic)**

STRUCTURED INTERVENTION PLANNING for ACADEMIC CONCERNS	25-minute meeting	35-minute meeting	50-minute meeting
Step 1 COLLECT BACKGROUND INFORMATION	6 min.	8 min.	10 min.
Step 2 IDENTIFY THE PROBLEM AND SET GOALS	3 min.	5 min.	9 min.
Step 3 BRAINSTORM PROACTIVE STRATEGIES	8 min.	10 min.	12 min.
Step 4 CREATE THE PLAN	5 min.	7 min.	10 min.
Step 5 FINAL DETAILS: EVALUATION AND SUPPORT	3 min.	5 min.	9 min.

Adapted from *B-RTI: Behavioral response to intervention: Creating a continuum of problem-solving and support* (Sprick, Booher, & Garrison, 2009)

beneficial for the Coach to read through those chapters—or even conduct professional development training for teachers on the chapters' content—before participating in a 25-minute team meeting for student academic concerns.

- You will notice that the 25-minute team problem-solving process for academic concerns has fewer steps than the process for behavior concerns. This is due in part to the fact that teachers who bring student academic concerns to the problem-solving team need to collect relevant data before the meeting to share with team members.

PRIOR TO MEETING

- Teacher conducts informal assessments, including running records, reading inventories, oral reading fluency checks, or other relevant assessments in the academic area of concern (e.g., math, spelling). Teacher brings copies to the team meeting.

- Teacher collects and analyzes student work samples. Teacher brings copies to the team meeting.

- Teacher conducts a 1:1 diagnostic teaching session with the student to assess the student's skills and school success strategies. The teacher observes the student while the student completes an academic task (e.g., reading a passage and answering questions about the passage content, calculating a series of math problems, writing a paragraph, describing how he or she would study for a test). Teacher brings observation notes to the team meeting.

- Contact parent(s) or guardian(s) as school policy or the situation requires.

STEP 1: COLLECT BACKGROUND INFORMATION

The teacher begins by describing the academic concern she has about the student and presents information she collected prior to the meeting. The teacher also describes the student's academic strengths. If the team believes that more information is needed, the Leader should stop the meeting and reschedule.

STEP 2: IDENTIFY THE PROBLEM AND SET GOALS

The team works with the teacher to narrow the scope of the problem, if necessary, and to identify one to three goals.

STEP 3: BRAINSTORM PROACTIVE STRATEGIES

The team brainstorms ideas for how to help the student meet the identified goals. Ideas may include

- changes in classroom structure and organization, including how material is presented and assessed;
- instruction or intervention to address the student's academic or learning challenges; and
- accommodations for adjusting the amount or difficulty of the student's workload.

The team brainstorms ideas for how to encourage the student to increase responsible academic behaviors. The Leader shall elicit as many ideas as possible from all meeting attendees. Avoid discussing, criticizing, or dismissing ideas as they come up—or promoting your own ideas as being the best.

STEP 4: CREATE THE PLAN

This step is identical to Step 6 in Team Problem Solving: Student Behavior Concerns.

STEP 5: FINAL DETAILS: EVALUATION AND SUPPORT

This step is identical to Step 7 in Team Problem Solving: Student Behavior Concerns.

Summary

Student-Focused Coaches use the Collaborative Planning process as one of their key strategies for establishing and maintaining a sense of trust and shared purpose with their colleagues as well as to develop plans to help students be more successful in school. Whether Coaches use the longer process for working with a single teacher or help implement the structured 25-minute problem-solving process for teams, these methods can help everyone at a school work together as a team of dedicated and effective professional educators.

4

DESIGNING ACADEMIC INTERVENTIONS FOR STUDENTS WITH READING DIFFICULTIES

Student-Focused Coaches engage in Collaborative Planning with teachers when students are not making enough progress in reading. In this chapter, we will provide a framework to guide Reading Coaches as they work with teachers to develop appropriate strategies for promoting student progress.

Three Student-Support Approaches

First, it's important to clarify the differences among three approaches teachers take to support students with reading difficulties. Each approach is very important, but it is essential that Coaches—and teachers—understand the differences among them. In various sources, these approaches may be given different names, but we will refer to them as they are described in the next section:

- *Accommodations* to enable students with reading difficulties to access grade-level text and content-area concepts

- *Adaptations* of instruction to successfully teach students with learning problems

- *Intensive reading intervention* programs

The term *intensive reading intervention* may be confusing, since SFC Coaches also talk about designing "interventions" as part of the Collaborative Planning process. We will discuss only intensive reading intervention *programs* briefly in one section of this chapter. Otherwise, when we use the word *interventions*, we will be referring to the special approaches and strategies that a Coach and teacher (or group of teachers) decide to use to address a student's problem related to reading.

ACCOMMODATIONS

Individualized educational programs (IEPs) for students who receive special education services often include lists of accommodations, which may include shortening assignments, giving extra time for completion of assignments, and other similar adjustments. Accommodations for students with reading difficulties may include giving oral (instead of written) tests, assigning a peer reader for content-area text, having the teacher read text orally, listening to tape-recorded text, or other strategies designed to give students access to the ideas in text. These accommodations are necessary and important; if they are found in a student's IEP, by law teachers must provide the accommodations when needed. Students who qualify for Section 504 of the Rehabilitation Act of 1973—a national civil rights law that prohibits discrimination on the basis of disabilities, including learning difficulties—also have a right to accommodations. Consider accommodations as similar to allowing a student with a broken leg to use crutches or to providing a wheelchair ramp so that a student with physical disabilities can access the school building. We wouldn't consider it unfair for a student to use crutches when he needs them, and it's not unfair for students with reading disabilities to be provided with accommodations so that they can access ideas in text.

Students with reading problems who have not been officially identified as having learning disabilities also benefit from accommodations, especially when they are asked to read content-area text that is above their instructional reading levels. When struggling readers are frequently asked to read frustration-level text, they tend to develop very counter-productive strategies. They often guess at words they don't know, or skip them altogether. When reading aloud, they sometimes mumble, hoping no one will notice that they can't read the words. Some students will act out or misbehave so that they will be sent out of the room rather than face reading text that is too difficult for them.

Providing accommodations like the ones we have described can enable students to learn from text, show what they know on tests, keep their attention focused on learning tasks, and provide beneficial practice opportunities. Providing accommodations is not only the smart thing to do for instruction, it's the humane thing to do—and often, it's required by law.

ADAPTATIONS

Although accommodations are important, they are not enough for students with reading problems. If these students are going to actually improve their reading abilities, they need *instruction*. More than 20 years of high-quality research has demonstrated the characteristics of effective instruction for struggling readers. Several of these characteristics are described in Chapter 2 of *The Reading Coach* book, and we will summarize a few of them here.

When teachers make *purposeful changes* to their instruction *to make it more effective* for students with learning difficulties or differences, they are making *instructional adaptations*. To understand the need for adaptations, consider the fact that students who are performing below grade level can close the reading gap only if they learn *faster* than typically developing classmates. (When you are behind in a race, you have to run faster than those ahead of you if you want to catch up.) This is pretty humbling to think about—students who struggle to learn to read have to make faster progress than average readers. Progress *is* possible when struggling readers receive *more instruction*, *more efficient instruction*, and *more practice*.

INTENSIVE READING INTERVENTION PROGRAMS

Research conducted by Foorman, Francis, Fletcher, Schatschneider, and Mehta (1998) shows that classroom reading instruction that includes explicit instruction in phonemic awareness and phonics in a print-rich environment can help most at-risk readers achieve success. But for some students, even excellent classroom reading instruction isn't enough. These students need *intensive reading intervention programs*. Teachers or other highly trained adult practitioners provide intensive reading intervention when they deliver supplemental small-group instruction in addition to regular classroom reading instruction. Students with the most severe reading problems need the most intensive intervention. They need very explicit instruction that is targeted to their individual needs, delivered in very small groups, or even 1:2 or 1:1 ratios. It is imperative for Reading Coaches to become familiar with research-validated intervention programs that have a track record of effectiveness with students who are at risk for, or who already have, serious reading problems. (See Chapter 2 for further discussion of intensive reading intervention.)

Planning Instructional Adaptations

One approach a Reading Coach can take when addressing reading problems in a Collaborative Planning process is to talk about the different kinds of adaptations that teachers can make to their reading instruction. Bryant and Bryant (2003) and Bryant, Smith, and Bryant (2008) have developed a framework that can help teachers formulate different kinds of adaptations. Bryant et al. describe four categories of adaptations that teachers can implement:

1. Instructional content
2. Instructional activities
3. Delivery of instruction
4. Materials used in instruction

Table 4.1 illustrates these four caegories and lists several examples of adaptations a coach and a teacher could consider during Collaborative Planning.

A NOTE ABOUT INSTRUCTIONAL CONTENT

Instructional content is, simply put, what we teach—the purpose of the lesson, our instructional objectives. Teachers may teach *skills*, *strategies*, and *content*. *Skills* are things students learn to do. In basketball, students learn skills like dribbling the ball and shooting free-throws. In reading, students must learn skills such as associating letters with their sounds (e.g., saying the sound of the letter **b**) and blending these sounds to form words (i.e., "sounding out" words).

A *strategy* is a routine or plan of action that can be used to accomplish a goal or to work through difficulty. A winning basketball team has strategies, or plans, to help them take advantage of their opponents' weaknesses and overcome their opponents' strengths. In reading, students can

Table 4.1   **A Framework for Designing Instructional Adaptations**

Category of Adaptations	Definition	Examples
Instructional Content	*What the teacher teaches (instructional objectives)*	• Reading words with advanced vowel combinations (e.g., **ai, ough, eigh**) (skill) • A strategy (or step-by-step plan) for finding the main idea of a paragraph (strategy) • The meaning of the Latin root *spect* ("to look or see," as in **inspect**) (content) • A strategy for identifying unknown words when reading • A strategy for spelling unknown words when writing • Other objectives in phonemic awareness, phonics, fluency, vocabulary, and comprehension • Objectives determined by examining the results of diagnostic assessments • Objectives based on a clear instructional sequence (systematic instruction), with potentially confusing elements separated (e.g., teaching the letters **b** and **d** several weeks apart so that students can master one before learning the other) • Controlling how much new information is introduced at one time so that students can master it • Reteaching skills, strategies, and content when progress monitoring and diagnostic assessments suggest a need
Instructional Activities	*What the teacher and students do (instructional lessons and activities implemented to address the objectives)*	• Directly teaching the most common sound of the letter **r** • Having students practice together saying the separate sounds in words (phonemic awareness) • Providing feedback as students apply word-study skills while reading orally • Planning activities that require active student involvement, allowing minimum time for students to sit and listen passively • Teaching a lesson on a comprehension strategy or skill from the core reading program • Planning partner-reading rather than round-robin reading to increase each student's active reading practice
Delivery of Instruction	*How the teacher teaches the lessons and implements the activities*	• Using various instructional groupings (e.g., large groups, small groups, student pairs) for different purposes • Providing clear modeling of skills and strategies • Providing both examples and nonexamples to clarify vocabulary words • Providing a lot of guided practice with effective feedback and instructional scaffolding • Breaking down directions into small steps • Providing independent practice with careful monitoring and feedback • Increasing the amount of specific positive feedback to students that is directly related to reading (rather than behavior) • Providing cumulative practice of previously learned skills together with newly learned skills • Using appropriate lesson pacing • Reducing "teacher talk" in small-group lessons to increase opportunities for students to actively respond

Table 4.1   **A Framework for Designing Instructional Adaptations (*cont'd.*)**

Category of Adaptations	Definition	Examples
		• Focusing on increasing the number of a student's accurate responses during small-group lessons by providing appropriate instruction, increasing active involvement, organizing materials to reduce downtime, providing scaffolding, etc.
Materials Used in Instruction	*Things the teacher uses*	• Magnetic letters or letter tiles to build or deconstruct words • Individual white boards to practice writing words • Word cards for word-sorting activities • Pictures or objects to illustrate vocabulary words • Graphic organizers to support comprehension and increase active involvement in comprehension lessons • Decodable text • Instructional-level text

Adapted from Bryant and Bryant (2003) and Bryant, Smith, and Bryant (2008)

be taught strategies for reading multisyllabic words, for spelling unknown words, and for writing summaries of paragraphs, among other kinds of strategies. Finally, students must learn *concepts*, or ideas, such as learning the meanings of common prefixes, suffixes, and roots to help them determine the meanings of unfamiliar words.

When making adaptations to instructional content, teachers should take care not to water-down instruction for students with reading problems. As an example, let's say Kiera and Thomas are students with word-reading difficulties in Mrs. Johnson's fifth-grade classroom. Both students need instruction in a strategy for reading multisyllabic words and in the skill of producing the sounds of vowel combinations (e.g., **ea**, **ai**, **ay**). At the same time, these students also need instruction in comprehending grade-level text and learning advanced vocabulary words. Mrs. Johnson may teach large-group comprehension and vocabulary lessons with accommodations (like peer readers) to help Kiera and Thomas access the grade-level text. Mrs. Johnson may also provide daily small-group instruction designed to teach the two students the word-identification skills and strategies they need to learn. It is important that Mrs. Johnson not excuse Kiera and Thomas from learning advanced comprehension and vocabulary skills because they have problems reading words in fifth-grade text.

A NOTE ABOUT INSTRUCTIONAL ACTIVITIES

It is important that teachers recognize the difference between *teaching activities* and *practice activities*:

• *Teaching activities* provide instruction any time a new skill, sight word, phonics element, or procedure is introduced or retaught.

- *Practice activities* provide reinforcement of skills and elements that have already been taught.

For struggling learners, it is imperative that teachers not skimp on teaching activities. For example, sometimes teachers have students complete worksheets on finding the main idea of a paragraph, but never teach students *how* to find the main idea. Students with learning difficulties need to have strategies like this modeled for them through a think-aloud. This instruction may be followed by guided practice by using a graphic organizer to scaffold their understanding of the strategy.

It's equally important to provide plenty of practice activities. Students can practice basic phonemic awareness and phonics skills using a variety of hands-on formats such as those in the "Adaptations for Trisha" scenario, following. Teachers should provide support, scaffolding, and feedback as students apply skills and strategies while reading and writing meaningful text.

Balancing Instruction, Practice, and Application

Students with reading difficulties generally benefit from explicit instruction, extended opportunities for practice, and plenty of time for applying skills and strategies as they read connected text with feedback from the teacher or some other person. How much time should be devoted to each of these activities?

As an example, in a research-validated first grade reading intervention approach called *Responsive Reading Instruction* (Denton & Hocker, 2006) teachers provide 40 minutes of small-group supplemental reading instruction every day. During each intervention lesson, students receive 10 minutes of direct instruction and practice in phonemic awareness, phonics, and word study. During this time they learn new skills and strategies and practice them in isolation (e.g., reading words in lists, spelling words, performing phonemic awareness tasks). During this 10-minute segment, teachers implement three to five brief instructional and/or practice activities, with most of the time devoted to practicing skills that were previously introduced, often by using game-like practice activities. (Note that these are *not* really games, but brief, hands-on, *purposeful activities* designed to actively involve students in practicing key skills.)

One example game activity: Students play a timed, flash-card word-reading game in which they try to "beat the teacher" by correctly identifying high-frequency words in 1–3 seconds. (The time limit starts at 3 seconds and then is decreased until students can read the words automatically.) If a student correctly reads the word on the flash card in the allotted time, the teacher places the card on the "Student" pile, which will serve the entire group. If a student incorrectly reads a word or exceeds the time limit, the student places the flash card on the "Teacher" pile. At the end of the game, the teacher counts the flash cards in both piles to determine the winner. Then, the teacher provides direct instruction and practice on the words that students missed (the cards in the "Teacher" pile).

During the second 10-minute segment of Responsive Reading Instruction, students practice repeated reading of instructional or independent-level text (and sometimes receive diagnostic assessments). This is followed by 10 minutes of reading unfamiliar text while the teacher provides feedback and scaffolding to support students as they apply new skills and strategies. This segment also includes comprehension skill instruction such as identifying components of story structure. In the final 10 minutes of the lesson, students compose a sentence in response to the teacher's question about the story they just read. With the teacher's support, students use sound analysis and their knowledge of spelling patterns to write the sentence correctly in their journals. Through this process, they apply phonemic awareness skills and knowledge of sound-to-print matching. The Responsive Reading Instruction sequence has been shown to be highly engaging to young students with reading difficulties and to support positive outcomes. It is only one example of an approach that includes explicit instruction, practice, and application in text reading and writing.

Using the Adaptation Framework in the Collaborative Planning Process

As a Coach and teacher work through the SFC Collaborative Planning process, they can use the adaptation framework in *Table 4.1* to think about instructional changes the teacher can make that may result in better outcomes for students. Some changes are small and don't require a lot of extra teacher time and work, but these may not always be enough to address the problem. Teachers may need to provide a small group of students with daily targeted instruction to accelerate their progress so they can catch up with their classmates. In these small groups, teachers often need to use *all four categories* of adaptations. Teachers adapt instructional content by basing their objectives on student assessment results. They adapt instructional activities by increasing active student involvement and planning extended practice activities. They adapt the delivery of instruction by making it more explicit, providing appropriate scaffolding and feedback, etc. Finally, they adapt the materials they use by including manipulatives and instructional-level text. The extent of adaptation needed is determined by the severity and nature of students' reading difficulties.

A SCENARIO: ADAPTATIONS FOR TRISHA

A first-grade student named Trisha is in Mrs. Garcia's class. It's January, and Trisha's benchmark test shows that she has made little progress in reading development so far this school year. On an assessment of oral reading fluency using grade-level text, Trisha's score was just 8 words correct per minute (wcpm), and she read the passage with only 78% accuracy. Mrs. Garcia and the Reading Coach address Trisha's lack of progress using the Collaborative Planning process. They define Trisha's problems as follows:

- Trisha has severe problems in accurately and fluently reading words in text.
- These problems seem to be related to difficulty in applying skills and strategies effectively while reading text.

- Although Trisha knows many letter-sounds and high-frequency words, she tends to guess unfamiliar words when she reads, often using only the first one or two letters in the words.

- Sometimes Trisha guesses nonsense words, and she fails to self-correct when her mistakes don't make sense.

Mrs. Garcia and the Reading Coach meet to develop a plan to address Trisha's problems. They set a goal that in four weeks Trisha will read grade-level passages at a minimum of 16 wcpm with at least 90% accuracy. Trisha's progress will be monitored with weekly assessments.

To assist in making adaptations, they refer to the book *Responsive Reading Instruction* (Denton & Hocker, 2006). They decide that Mrs. Garcia will make the following adaptations:

1. **Instructional Content**

   In Trisha's small-group reading instruction, which Mrs. Garcia provides as part of her regular daily classroom reading program, Trisha will receive direct instruction in
   - the letter-sound correspondences she tends to confuse;
   - sounding out words smoothly; and
   - a three-part strategy for reading unknown words in text described in the *Responsive Reading Instruction* book:
     a. "Look for parts of the word that you know." (In the beginning, this may be just one or two letters; later, it may be familiar rimes or syllable patterns, or prefixes and suffixes.)
     b. "Sound out the word by saying it slowly and smoothly."
     c. "Check it by putting the word back into the sentence and reading to be sure it makes sense."

2. **Instructional Activities**

   To teach these objectives, Mrs. Garcia will use activities described in the *Responsive Reading Instruction* book:
   - *Teaching Letter-Sounds:* Explicitly teaching new letter-sounds by modeling the sound, providing guided and independent small-group practice, and providing individual independent practice; then practicing the sound mixed in with previously learned sounds.
   - *The Pick up the Letter Game:* Practicing letter-sound correspondences by selecting magnetic letters representing sounds dictated by the teacher from a group of magnetic letters ("Pick up the letter that makes this sound: /f/.").
   - *Teaching Sounding Out:* Explicitly modeling and providing practice in sounding out words smoothly.
   - *The Point Game:* Practicing sounding out words. Students take turns sounding out words presented by the teacher and receive a point for each word they sound out correctly. The teacher purposefully scaffolds students and continues around the group until each child has 2–3 points. (The game normally ends in a tie, which doesn't seem to bother first graders.)
   - *Modeling and Teaching the Word Reading Strategy:* Using activities for teaching and prompting the use of the three-part strategy for reading unknown words in text, as described previously.

- *Teaching Self-Monitoring in Text Reading:* Modeling and prompting students to notice when they make errors and to self-correct them.

3. **Delivery of Instruction**

   Implementing the activities described in the *Responsive Reading Instruction* book will make the instruction explicit, provide many opportunities for practice, and increase hands-on active involvement.

4. **Instructional Materials**

   For the daily small-group lessons, Mrs. Garcia will provide text at Trisha's instructional reading level and use flash cards, individual white boards, and magnetic letters on individual trays.

The Reading Coach will support Mrs. Garcia by co-planning small group lessons, modeling the activities, and helping Mrs. Garcia find the materials she needs. The Coach will check in with Mrs. Garcia frequently and provide her with modeling as needed.

The End of Trisha's Story

Trisha learned to sound out words rather than guessing and to check to be sure that what she is reading makes sense. Mrs. Garcia learned some powerful strategies that she can use to provide effective instruction to other students. Of course, real-life endings are not always this perfect, but using the adaptation framework may help teachers and Coaches make changes to instruction that result in improved outcomes for students, which is the ultimate goal of the Reading Coach.

Summary

It can be helpful to think about three approaches to supporting struggling readers: providing modifications, adaptations, and intensive reading intervention programs. Each of these approaches is important and necessary. In this chapter, we focused particularly on a framework that can guide teachers as they adapt their classroom instruction to support the reading development of struggling students. Coaches may teach this adaptation framework in professional development sessions or grade-level meetings and model different adaptation strategies, including instructional activities like those described in the scenario. This can give teachers and Coaches a common language and starting point when they work together in the Collaborative Planning process.

5

COLLABORATIVE PLANNING FOR STUDENT BEHAVIOR CONCERNS

Reading Coaches work with their colleagues in a variety of ways to help them provide the best reading instruction possible to their students. Student-Focused Coaching (SFC) is categorized into three roles: Facilitator, Collaborative Problem Solver, and Teacher-Learner. In all of these roles, the primary focus of the Coach's work should be on students' academic success.

The SAILS model that we developed in *The Reading Coach* book is based on research that examined how even highly challenged schools help their students succeed academically. We believe that Coaches have a greater likelihood of success if they work within a system that addresses the five SAILS components: Standards, Assessments, Instruction and Intervention, Leadership, and Sustained Schoolwide Commitment.

However, SAILS only addresses the academic side of coaching. The SAILS model must be "launched" into a school environment where every student feels safe and the atmosphere of the school and each classroom is positive and supportive. When we think about how academics and behavior fit together in a school, we see that behavior is the foundation for academic achievement—or perhaps the flip side of the coin of student success.

When *Might* Reading Coaches Need to Help With Behavior Concerns?

Every Coach eventually encounters situations in which the student's *behavior* must be addressed in order to help a teacher improve student learning. There are many situations where a Reading Coach might be asked to work with a colleague regarding a student's behavior. Here are three possible scenarios:

1. Tony is in kindergarten. He is a gregarious and happy child with good language skills and an abundance of curiosity about his surroundings. His teacher is having difficulty getting Tony to pay attention to her literacy lessons. Tony has been unable to complete any of the practice activities—copying letters, using magnetic letters to form words, using the listening center, etc.—she has assigned to the students. Tony's teacher is certain that he can do the work, but he just can't seem to settle down and stay focused.

2. Kayla is a fourth-grade student. Her records indicate that she has been performing at least at an average level in all academic areas since she started school. Her reading and language arts work in fourth grade started off well, but suddenly Kayla has stopped turning in homework, doesn't complete work in class, and her reading work seems to have become much more difficult for her.

3. Jacob is a seventh-grade student. He has been struggling with reading since he was in first grade and currently reads at about a fourth-grade level. He has been targeted to receive help in the school's reading intervention program and has been assigned to attend a reading lab for one period each day. The lab teacher as well as some of Jacob's content teachers have concerns that Jacob's attendance is poor and, when he is in class, he talks back to the teachers, doesn't follow directions, and refuses to do the work.

Do any of these stories sound familiar to you? If you were the Reading Coach in these schools, what would be your response if Tony's—or Kayla's or Jacob's—teacher approached you for help? In each case, unless the student's behavior improves, it is unlikely that even the best instruction or intervention will be successful.

Should a Reading Coach Work With Teachers on Behavioral Concerns?

If you are currently a Reading Coach or have ever been a classroom teacher, it is likely that the stories of Tony, Kayla, and Jacob are indeed familiar to you. You may have worked with students similar to them or with students who have more serious behavioral or emotional issues. Every educator is painfully aware that there are many students who have behavioral challenges, often along with serious academic concerns. In fact, researchers have made a strong case that in some cases, students' behavioral problems are caused by their academic struggles. It may be less punishing and less humiliating for a student such as Jacob to avoid doing difficult or confusing assigned work by skipping school, refusing to complete assignments, or causing problems that distract from his academic deficits. From the perspective of a struggling reader, it may be easier to be labeled "bad" than "stupid."

So then the question remains: If a teacher contacts a Reading Coach about a student's behavioral concerns, *should* the Coach try to help? Or, is it acceptable for a Coach to draw a line by stating, "I'm a Reading Coach. I don't 'do' behavior"?

Ultimately, answering that question comes down to an individual decision. We know of no general rule about whether a Reading Coach should or should not assist a teacher with a student's behavioral concern. It is likely, however, that some individual states, districts, or schools may have established policies for this issue.

To help *you* make your own decision in this matter, we look to the guidelines for defining roles, responsibilities, and ethical standards for performance published by coaching researchers and by relevant professional organizations. Dr. Jan Dole (2004) broadly defines a Reading

Coach as someone who "supports teachers in their daily work" (p. 462). One could certainly make the case that helping students to responsibly manage their own behaviors while in school is within the "daily work" of most teachers. Dole's definition could be viewed as one vote for the Coach helping his or her colleagues with behavioral concerns.

The National Education Association (NEA) published a list of professional ethics in 1975 that includes the statement "[Educators] shall make reasonable effort to protect the student from conditions harmful to learning or to health and safety." It could be argued that the behaviors exhibited by Tony, Kayla, and Jacob are harmful to their learning. Following these guidelines from the NEA, one might conclude that teachers and Coaches *should* collaborate to address behavioral concerns, which could be another vote for having Coaches help teachers with students' challenging behaviors.

An important caveat comes from the Council for Exceptional Children (CEC) in 2003. In their detailed publication of the ethical standards for special educators, the CEC states: "Professionals practice only in areas of exceptionality, at age levels, and in program models for which they are prepared by their training and/or experience" (p. 4). This statement should serve as an important reminder to Coaches who *do* decide to work with their colleagues regarding students' behavioral concerns. To maintain ethical professional standards, Coaches must inform themselves about best practices in dealing with behavioral concerns *before* attempting to work in this area. All Coaches must be fully aware of the limits of their own expertise and of the importance of providing the best possible services to students in this or in any area. Reading Coaches must be willing to seek assistance from and collaborate with behavioral specialists, special educators, school counselors, school psychologists, social workers, nurses, and other relevant professionals when working with colleagues in the area of student behavior and emotional well-being.

The remainder of this chapter is designed to provide some background knowledge, references, and resources for Coaches who will undertake collaboration regarding students' behavior in the course of their work.

What Is Research-Supported Best Practice in Behavior Management and Intervention?

Psychologists have been studying human behavior for hundreds of years. From this extensive scientific knowledge base, parents and educators have learned a lot about how to help children develop positive, pro-social behaviors, as well as how to intervene when a child, youth or adolescent is having difficulty managing his or her own behaviors. This is essential knowledge for educators, because we can use this information to help all students learn how to interact and conduct themselves successfully in the world of school, home, and community.

We have found three sources particularly helpful—and practical—for guiding educators in this key area. One is Sopris West Educational Services (http://www.sopriswest.com), which publishes a vast number of resources related to positive school climate, safe schools, and social skills. A second helpful source is the work of Dr. George Sugai from the University of Connecticut and Dr. Rob Horner from the University of Oregon (Sugai & Horner, 2007), who developed the widely used systems-level model called Positive Behavioral Interventions and Supports (PBIS), which we will discuss in the next section. The third source is the work of Dr. Randy Sprick and his colleagues (Sprick, Booher, & Garrison, 2009; Sprick, Garrison, & Howard, 1998) at Safe & Civil Schools.

POSITIVE BEHAVIORAL INTERVENTIONS AND SUPPORTS (PBIS)—PREVENTION AND INTERVENTION

The Office of Special Education Programs (OSEP) has established an online Technical Assistance Center on Positive Behavioral Interventions and Supports (PBIS). The purpose of this Center is to provide educators with access to the research-based PBIS model developed by Sugai and Horner (Sugai & Horner, 2007) to both prevent behavior problems from occurring in the first place and to intervene successfully if such problems develop. The key features of PBIS are listed in an undated brochure published by the U.S. Office of Special Education Programs:

- Teach behavioral expectations to all students.
- Establish schoolwide behavioral expectations.
- Develop a continuum of consequences for violations of the expectations.
- Acknowledge appropriate behavior.
- Use data for continuous decision-making.
- Provide support for students with chronic problem behavior.

The PBIS model is a systems approach to establishing the social culture and behavioral supports needed for all students in a school to achieve both social and academic success. It is not a packaged curriculum, but rather an approach that defines core elements that can be achieved through a variety of strategies. There are three tiers in the model:

- **Tier 1: Primary Prevention**—School- and classroom-wide systems for all students, staff, and settings.
- **Tier 2: Secondary Prevention**—Specialized group systems for students with at-risk behavior (approximately 15% of students).
- **Tier 3: Tertiary Prevention**—Individualized systems for students with high-risk behavior (approximately 5% of students).

The PBIS Technical Assistance Center Web site (http://www.pbis.org) describes the three tiers of PBIS as follows.

Tier 1: Primary Prevention involves systemwide efforts to prevent problems from developing. Primary Prevention begins with having a school develop and teach rules, routines, and physical

Figure 5.1 **Three-Tier PBIS Model**
From the Office of Special Education Programs (OSEP) Technical Assistance Center on Positive Behavioral Interventions and Supports (PBIS)

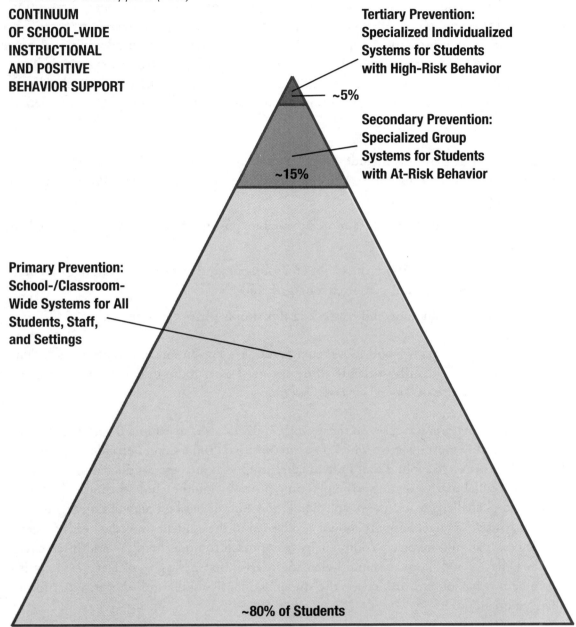

CONTINUUM OF SCHOOL-WIDE INSTRUCTIONAL AND POSITIVE BEHAVIOR SUPPORT

Tertiary Prevention: Specialized Individualized Systems for Students with High-Risk Behavior

~5%

Secondary Prevention: Specialized Group Systems for Students with At-Risk Behavior

~15%

Primary Prevention: School-/Classroom-Wide Systems for All Students, Staff, and Settings

~80% of Students

arrangements to prevent initial occurrences of problem behaviors. For example, PBIS developers suggest that to prevent injuries to students caused by running in hallways, schools may

- establish and teach the rule "Walk in the hallways";
- create a routine in which staff position themselves in the hallways during transition times to supervise the movement of students; and/or
- alter the physical arrangement, such as making sure that an adult is with any group of students when they are in the hallways.

The research on PBIS has shown that Primary Prevention, through positive behavior support, works for more than 80% of all students. Of course, it won't take care of *all* behavior problems. For a variety of reasons, some students just don't respond to Primary Prevention efforts. For those students, PBIS recommends that schools use *Tier 2: Secondary Prevention*, which provides intensive, targeted interventions to help students who need additional support. Secondary Prevention is typically provided in small groups of ten or fewer students or as individualized intervention strategies. PBIS research documents that typical school personnel can implement targeted interventions with positive effects on up to 67% of referred students.

Specific Tier 2 interventions include practices such as "social skills club," "check in/check out," and the Behavior Education Plan. Individual plans at the Secondary Prevention level include a range of options, such as

- teaching students how to use more acceptable, positive behaviors to replace problem behaviors;

- rearranging the classroom or school environment so that problems can be prevented and desirable behaviors can be encouraged; and

- monitoring, evaluating, and reassessing this simple plan over time.

Observing how students respond to targeted Secondary Prevention interventions is recommended as a way to identify students who may need even more intensive, individualized intervention assistance in *Tier 3: Tertiary Prevention*.

Tier 3: Tertiary Prevention focuses on the needs of individuals who exhibited patterns of problem behavior. It is most effective when there are positive Primary and Secondary systems in place. PBIS research has found that individualized supports are best conducted in a comprehensive and collaborative manner. The planning process should include the individual with the behavioral challenges and the people who know him or her best all working together to promote positive change. Support should be tailored to the student's specific needs and circumstances. It should involve a comprehensive approach to understanding and intervening with the behavior and should use multi-element interventions. The goal of Tier 3 is to diminish problem behavior and to increase the student's adaptive skills and opportunities for an enhanced quality of life.

Tertiary Prevention includes a range of options similar to Secondary group strategies but implemented for an individual student. In some cases, a plan may need to include emergency procedures to ensure safety and rapid de-escalation of severe episodes (this is required when the behavior is dangerous to the student or others), or even significant placement changes to a specialized classroom or even a different school.

The PBIS systems approach is one that can inform the work of school leaders at a district or school level. But how should the three tiers be used in classroom settings? What ideas could a Coach share with colleagues who want help organizing and managing their classrooms? What ideas or strategies can we offer to Tony, Kayla, or Jacob's teacher?

For these answers, we turn to the work of Dr. Randy Sprick and colleagues. They have created a library of useful resources and tools for educators to help develop effective systems for teaching students how to develop responsible behaviors. (For a partial listing of these resources, see Books and Articles in the *References* section.) Sprick et al. base their work on research conducted over the past decades. From that research, they developed a set of guidelines and principles for teachers who want their classrooms to be safe, positive, and effective learning environments for all their students (Sprick, Garrison, & Howard, 1998). To accomplish these kinds of classrooms, teachers must

- establish smooth, efficient classroom routines;
- interact with students in positive, caring ways;
- provide incentives, recognition, and rewards to promote excellence; and
- set clear standards for classroom behavior and apply them fairly and consistently.

Establishing smooth, efficient classroom routines

Teachers need to set up procedures that maximize productive instructional time and help students effectively manage their own social behaviors. These management procedures can be used in the classrooms of very young children up through the classrooms of graduate students! Begin by setting up a daily instructional schedule that allows time for whole class and small group instruction, transitions, breaks, etc. Set up a paper management system so students know where to find work assignments and where to put them when they have been completed. This system should also work for notes to/from home, lunch money, homework, etc. Assign jobs to students so they are responsible for the time-consuming tasks that keep the teacher from focusing on planning and delivering instruction. These jobs can range from Paper Monitor to Sound Level Monitor to Counselor—who addresses the interpersonal problems that may arise between students while the teacher is teaching. The teacher needs to *teach* her students how to do these jobs and how to manage their papers and other materials. You can find helpful ideas and a week-by-week coaching plan for these ideas in the book *Differentiated Instruction: Grouping for Success* (Gibson & Hasbrouck, 2008).

Interacting with students in positive, caring ways

The classroom environment needs to be well organized and efficient, but it must also be a place where students feel safe and valued. Educators work hard to keep students *physically* safe while they are involved in school-related activities, but we must work just has hard to keep our students *psychologically* safe. Learning will be limited or even prevented if students feel belittled, ridiculed, or ignored. Sprick et al. (1998) suggest that teachers work hard to establish a positive relationship with each student and advises teachers to strive for a ratio of 3:1 positive-to-negative comments for every student. Maintaining this ratio demonstrates to students that they do not have to misbehave to get adult attention and that the teacher is actively interested in each student as person and notices his or her successes. Sprick et al. also suggest making positive comments that are non-contingent. For example, greeting each student as he or she arrives in class or saying, "Hi Maria. How are you today?" when you see a student in the hallway. These comments add to the total ratio on the positive side and help maintain a safe and positive environment.

Providing incentives, recognition, and rewards to promote excellence

Every teacher would like students to want to learn and achieve success simply for the love of learning. Along the way to that goal, however, we know that most human beings respond to positive reinforcement for their efforts. Along with organizing a classroom and ensuring that it is a physically and psychologically safe and positive environment for learning, teachers need to look for ways to inspire and compensate appropriate behaviors. This doesn't mean you need to give candy or prizes to students for correct responses! A smile and "Good job, Lonnie!" can inspire students to keep trying and improving. Teachers need to use incentives and rewards that are reasonable and age-appropriate.

Setting clear standards for classroom behavior and applying them fairly and consistently

Teachers need to think carefully about what they actually want students to do in the classroom so that these expectations can be implemented consistently. Some commonly suggested guidelines include:

- Establish rules and procedures *the first day of school.* Students need to know your expectations for behavior and daily classroom procedures and routines right away.

- Clearly define the rules, and keep them short and simple. Students may need a model of what you expect for them to achieve the desired result. For example, what do you mean by "arrive to class on time"? Is it acceptable for a student to run in the room as the bell is ringing, dive for his chair (knocking it over in the process, of course), and land on the floor just as the bell stops ringing? Probably not, but this has to be clearly spelled out for students who like to test the limits or who need very concrete examples to follow. Have students provide examples and non-examples of this behavior to make sure there is a shared understanding between teacher and students.

- Give students a voice in establishing classroom rules. This gives them more ownership in the process and makes them more likely to hold each other accountable.

- Make rules positive. Try stating the class rules in terms such as, "Respect your property and the property of others."

- Keep the list of rules short, perhaps three to five rules. Students are more likely to remember a short list of general rules than a long list of specific ones. Be sure the rules cover all the key issues that need to be addressed for guiding students to make responsible choices with their behavior.

- Enforce the rules consistently. You can develop a wonderful set of classroom rules, but if they aren't enforced completely and consistently, they will soon become useless. If students see they can break rules with no consequences or if the rules are applied inconsistently, they will soon ignore them.

Scenario for Behavior Interventions

Remember Jacob, the seventh-grader? We previously introduced him as a student who has been struggling with reading since he was in first grade and currently reads at about a fourth-grade level. Jacob has been placed in a reading lab for daily intervention, and his content teachers are also working on ways to help Jacob improve his reading and writing skills. However, his teachers have all expressed concern about Jacob's attendance and the inappropriate, irresponsible behaviors that he is demonstrating in and outside of the classroom: talking back to teachers, refusing to do work, and being generally uncooperative. Several teachers have described Jacob as a "troublemaker."

> Jacob's reading lab teacher, Ms. Wilson, asks the Reading Coach for help with Jacob. She says that Jacob verbally disrupts the class, shows physical aggression to other students, and has even thrown items from time to time. The Coach talks to Ms. Wilson about doing either developing a Collaborative Plan together, using the Systematic Problem Solving strategy or possibly setting up a team meeting using the 25-minute strategy. (See details about both these options in Chapter 3, "Problem Solving Within SFC.") Ms. Wilson has worked with the Coach previously on a Collaborative Plan and has also found success in the 25-minute process. For this case they decide to begin the process with just the two of them—to get a handle on the situation—and then involve Jacob's other teachers for team planning. They begin with a Phase 1: Problem Presentation conversation, discussing the presenting problem. (Adapted from "The Transitional Life of Riley McKinley" from the PBIS Technical Assistance Center website at http://www.pbis.org.)

Ms. Wilson says that Jacob is in her fourth period reading lab. There are 11 students from grades 7 and 8 in that class. Jacob misses at least one day per week, sometimes two. Jacob does best with hands-on activities but quits easily if an assignment involves reading or spelling. Jacob has a couple of friends in her class. Ms. Wilson has current academic assessment data that she shares with the Coach but they agree to keep the focus for now on just his behavior.

Ms. Wilson has tried to make contact with Jacob's home with no success. She has talked with some of Jacob's other teachers and reports that they see similar issues in their classes as well, but no one has seriously tried any specific intervention with Jacob. The Coach and Ms. Wilson agree that it would be helpful for the Coach to do some observations in Jacob's fourth period reading class to get a sense of current, baseline performance. The Coach suggests that an ABC observation of antecedents, behavior, and consequences would be helpful. (See *The Reading Coach* book for more information about this observation tool.) Ms. Wilson also agrees to try again to contact Jacob's parents to see if there may be some helpful information that they could provide. Ms. Wilson and the Coach end this meeting by setting a date for conducting the observations and a plan to get Jacob's other teachers together for using Collaborative Planning, starting with a 25-minute team-planning process.

Ms. Wilson and Jacob's other teachers decide to collaboratively address the challenges each one of them is having with Jacob. They decide to use the 35-minute version of the timed planning process, and they find a time to get together eight days later.

As the team gathers, the roles of Leader, Recorder, and Timekeeper are assigned. The Coach takes the role of Leader so other teachers—all of whom work with Jacob—can participate as fully as possible in the planning process.

STEP 1: BACKGROUND (7 MINUTES)

The teachers took turns sharing their concerns about Jacob's behavior in their own classrooms. The patterns of missed classes, talking back to teachers, and throwing objects seems common to every class. No one has tried any specific behavior that has helped much. They also agree that Jacob's strengths are a friendly personality and good communication skills.

Ms. Wilson shared what she learned from talking with Jacob's mother, Mrs. Lamond: Jacob is the younger of two children; his sister is in high school. Jacob does not do much around the house because his sister tends to "baby" him and do any chores for him. Mrs. Lamond works full time as an accountant, and Mr. Lamond travels frequently out of state for his business. Mrs. Lamond admitted that mornings are quite chaotic and that Jacob's lack of organizational skills cause him to frequently have a "bad" morning. Mrs. Lamond also told Ms. Wilson that she and her husband have been worried about Jacob's academic and behavior problems for quite some time and are willing to work with the school on any plans they devise to help Jacob. Mrs. Lamond suggested that Jacob might work to earn a new video game to play at home.

The Coach shared the results from the ABC observation conducted one day in Ms. Wilson's fourth period reading lab. The observation seems to show that Jacob's outbursts or physical aggression occur to avoid doing work that is difficult or confusing for him. Sometimes, he behaves poorly to get attention from the teacher or other students. He also had difficulty during any transition from one activity to another.

STEP 2: PROBLEM AND GOAL (3 MINUTES)

The team decided to focus on reducing Jacob's talk-outs and physical outbursts. Jacob's teachers agreed on two goals: By the end of one month (1) Jacob will reduce his talk-outs to no more than one per period, and (2) Jacob will reduce his physical outbursts to zero. They are hopeful that the plan will also increase Jacob's attendance in their classes.

STEP 3: CORRECTIVE CONSEQUENCES (3 MINUTES)

After discussing the options of either (1) correcting or ignoring an irresponsible behavior, or (2) administering a consequence, the team decided to use a combination of precorrection and consequence. Jacob will lose points to use towards an earned privilege related to getting increased attention.

STEP 4: RESPONSIBLE AND IRRESPONSIBLE BEHAVIORS (6 MINUTES)

This step took a bit longer than the allotted six minutes. The Leader asked the team for permission to add one minute to this step when they got to the six-minute mark without reaching an agreement on a description of Jacob's problem behaviors. The team spent their time clearly defining a "talk-out" and "physical outbursts." The group eventually agreed to define a talk-out as a loud verbal sound or words that disturb the learning environment. A physical outburst was defined as when an object leaves Jacob's hands and lands at least 6 inches from him, or any part of Jacob's body comes in contact with another person with force.

STEP 5: PROACTIVE STRATEGIES (6 MINUTES)

The team brainstormed some ideas that would help Jacob get the attention he seemed to desire. They discussed letting Jacob be the class messenger, have some one-on-one time with a teacher, lead the weekly class discussion of weekend planning and debriefing, tutor in the elementary school next door, and work with an older male mentor. They also decided that Jacob needed to learn some ways of handling his anxiety and discussed some options for that. A couple of teachers shared a "secret signal" strategy that they had previously used that had been successful. This strategy allows a student to feel some control over a classroom situation and get help without causing any problems like yelling or fighting.

STEP 6: CREATE THE PLAN (4 MINUTES)

Jacob's teachers agreed to the following plan:

1. Jacob would learn a "secret signal" of moving his nametag to the left side of his desk when he needed a break. This way Jacob could tell his teacher that he didn't understand the new task and needed a break until he could get some assistance. Jacob would look at a book until the teacher could help him.

2. For transitions, the team agreed on several ways that Jacob could get more attention in a positive way:
   - Jacob was connected with a 16-year-old volunteer from the nearby high school who would serve as a mentor to Jacob. This volunteer student would meet with Jacob each day for 10–15 minutes in the morning and talk about what he did the night before and what was on his agenda for the day. This was designed to help Jacob make a smooth transition from home to school.
   - At the end of each school day, Jacob would meet with Ms. Wilson or the Reading Coach to talk about what homework he needed to get done that evening. Ms. Wilson or the

Coach would compliment him for filling out his assignment book and talk about any situations that arose during the day. They would look over his daily point chart.

- All the teachers agreed to keep an agenda posted on the board or overhead so that Jacob would know what activities were coming next.
- Jacob would start each period with four points. Points would be lost for talking out or physical outbursts. At the end of the day, Ms. Wilson or the Coach would add up the total points for the day with Jacob and award one additional point for meeting with them. There were a total of 25 points each day. At the end of the week, if Jacob had earned at least 100 points he could choose where his family would have their Sunday lunch together. At the end of one month, Jacob could exchange his points for a video game from his parents.

STEP 7: FINAL DETAILS (6 MINUTES)

The team used this time to wrap up final details such as the evaluation plan, how teachers would support each other in implementing the plan successfully, and identifying each person's responsibilities. Ms. Wilson agreed that she would discuss the plan with Jacob and his parents. The team scheduled a follow-up meeting for one month later.

After four weeks, the team met again. Jacob's teachers agreed they had seen very few disruptive outbursts and no physical aggression. Jacob is also attending school almost every day. A couple of teachers remarked that they had almost forgotten that Jacob had ever been a problem. The Coach had contacted Jacob's parents who also commented that they saw some improvements in Jacob's behavior and attitude at home. The Coach and Ms. Wilson now want to turn their attention to Jacob's reading challenges. They will schedule a time to meet to start the Collaborative Planning process again to address academic concerns.

Summary

A Reading Coach may work with colleagues who are facing challenging social behaviors in their students. There are many very powerful and positive strategies that adults can use to help students learn better ways of handling their frustrations and anxiety. When teachers learn to use these strategies effectively and consistently, students can make tremendous improvements in their behavior and their emotional well-being, which can then have a major impact on their academic performance.

6

STUDENT-FOCUSED CLASSROOM OBSERVATIONS

Reading Coaches are often called on to observe teachers while they instruct students. There are several good reasons to do this. For example, part of the Collaborative Planning process is gathering data to help define a problem, set goals, and develop interventions. Observations can also provide important data used to evaluate the effectiveness of solutions. These observations may focus on specific student behaviors, such as whether students are on-task and actively engaged in instruction.

Other observations are conducted as a component of professional development. Often, Coaches observe teachers and provide feedback to help them refine their skills. Some teachers are quite open to this kind of feedback, which can support them as they engage in guided and independent practice of recently learned instructional routines. For the Coach, however, it can be challenging to provide colleagues with feedback while establishing and maintaining truly collaborative relationships with them.

We will describe two strategies to address this situation. The first is conducting Student-Focused Observations (SFO), which are observations focused on the interactions between teachers and students (rather than directly on teachers themselves). The second is a procedure we call two-way observations.

Conducting Student-Focused Observations

One of the hallmarks of SFC is that teachers and Coaches focus together on students and their needs. Coaches keep the focus on students by examining the *interactions* between teachers and students during lesson observations, rather than looking only at teacher behaviors. In other words, the Coach (or another teacher) observes and provides feedback about how students respond to their teachers' decisions and behaviors—or how teachers respond to student behaviors. This approach is based, in part, on a conclusion reached by Joyce and Showers (1981), two pioneers in the field of educational coaching. In their decades spent observing the coaching process, Joyce and Showers determined that *it is less important that teachers receive feedback on how well they are executing a teaching strategy than on the quality of the instructional decisions they make as they integrate the strategy in different situations in pursuit of specific goals.* In other words, teachers need to learn more than *how* to implement new teaching approaches; they need to learn *when to apply* these approaches and *how to modify them* in response to student needs. At this level, teachers are able to engage in a continuous process of on-the-spot problem solving as they respond to the needs of their students.

THE STUDENT-FOCUSED OBSERVATION FORM

When conducting student-focused observations, we use the Student-Focused Observation (SFO) form (formerly known as the "Observation Non-Form" because of its simplicity). *Figure 6.1* shows a sample SFO form, and a blank copy of the form is provided in the *Appendix*. Essentially, this form is a piece of paper divided into two columns by a vertical line. There are spaces for essential information at the top of the page, such as the teacher's name, the date, and the observer's name. There is also a space to fill in the Observation Focus. The Observation Focus should be one or two characteristics of effective instruction (e.g., providing clear modeling, extending opportunities for practice, providing small-group instruction, providing students with appropriate positive and corrective feedback) that are the focus of the observation. (For more examples, look at some of the adaptations listed in *Table 4.1* in Chapter 4, "A Framework for Designing Instructional Adaptations.")

There are three important considerations in selecting the Observation Focus. First, be sure that it is an *observable teacher behavior*. For example, the goal "Mrs. Heinz will implement phonics instruction more confidently" needs to be reworked because it would be hard to observe and record each time the teacher felt more confident during a lesson! Second, be sure the Observation Focus is—well—*focused!* Think about how difficult it would be to observe and record *all* the details for an Observation Focus like "providing effective phonemic awareness instruction." It is more useful to focus on a particular *aspect* of the instruction, such as correctly modeling how to segment words or providing effective error correction and feedback. The third consideration in selecting an Observation Focus is that it should be *something that has been discussed* in professional development or that the Coach has modeled for the teacher. Observation directs the teacher's attention to something specific, so plan observations that focus on elements of instruction you emphasize in professional development. It is important to meet with the teacher before the observation to agree on the Observation Focus.

Below the information at the top of the SFO form, there are two columns, one labeled *Teacher Behaviors* and one labeled *Student Behaviors*. As you observe the teacher, record in the *Teacher Behaviors* column any instances when the teacher *does* implement the Observation Focus behavior (even if it is not perfectly implemented). Across from this description of the teacher behavior in the *Student Behaviors* column, record any observations about how the students responded. Be sure to record enough details about both the teacher and student behaviors so that you can relay what you saw to the teacher, even if you can't meet until one or two days later. Think of these notes as "snapshots" of instruction. Take care not to include judgments about the quality of the teacher's instruction. Stick to the facts: "When the teacher did ___ the students did ___."

Figure 6.1. **Sample Student-Focused Observation Form**

Student-Focused Observation Form

Teacher **Mr. Wright**   Grade or Class **1st Gr. Reading Small Group**   Date **2-13-09**

Coach **Mrs. Evans**   Start Time **9:00**   End Time **10:00**

Observation Focus **Providing Explicit Modeling of New Skills**

Teacher Behaviors	Student Behaviors
Directly taught the sound of the letter 'h.' When Justin had problems in the story with the word 'ham,' the teacher stopped him and modeled sounding out the word.	Justin answered correctly when shown the flash card with the letter 'h.' Justin was able to sound out the word 'ham' correctly after the teacher's model and continued reading. When he came to the word 'had,' first Justin said 'has,' but then he stopped to sound out the word ('had') and read it correctly.

Figure 6.1 provides an example of a completed SFO form. As you examine the form, please note that when you take notes during an observation you will probably use your own shorthand and not write with quite as much attention to sentence structure as we have done in the example. Of course, in the real world, students will not always respond as perfectly as Justin did in this scenario. In reality, Justin could have just as easily gotten the sound of the letter **h** wrong and failed to self-correct his error on the word **had**. Perhaps Mr. Wright didn't clearly demonstrate how to sound out the word for him. Regardless, the Coach should record *any indication* that (a) the teacher made an attempt to implement the Observation Focus, and (b) there was a positive response from one of the students.

Providing Feedback Using the SFO Form

It is very important that the SFO be followed as soon as possible with a debriefing meeting with the teacher. This meeting should occur without students present, when the teacher can focus on the discussion. At this meeting, the Coach describes the "snapshot of instruction" recorded on the SFO form. The beauty of this type of observation is that feedback (a) has a neutral, rather than critical, tone because the observer recorded only examples of the teacher implementing (or trying to implement) the Observation Focus; and (b) is a factual account of how students reacted, rather than a subjective quality judgment. Imagine how a teacher might feel when receiving each of the following kinds of feedback:

1. "You should model more clearly when a student makes a mistake."
2. "When you modeled how to sound out the word **ham**, Justin was able to successfully blend the sounds and read the word."

The second type of feedback is probably less threatening. Now, Mr. Wright may have missed five other chances to provide explicit modeling, but the fact that you noticed the one time he did model calls Mr. Wright's attention to two important things: (1) he *can* implement the strategy of modeling to provide feedback, and (2) when he does, it can help his students be more successful. These are two things you want a teacher to believe as they are both powerful motivators and the basis of successful interventions developed through Collaborative Planning.

The Two-Way Observation Procedure

If Mr. Wright is unlikely to provide explicit modeling during an observation, the procedure we just described may not work very well. In that case, we recommend a two-way observation,

Table 6.1   The Two-Way Observation Procedure

Step 1: The Coach and Teacher Co-Plan Two Lessons
• Together, the teacher and Coach plan two lessons to be taught on two successive days (or as close in time as possible).   • The Coach models the process of planning instruction targeted to student needs, based on assessment data and using appropriate materials.   • The Coach also models planning each component of effective instruction for struggling readers (e.g., having a clear, purposeful objective; modeling; guided practice; independent practice; opportunities to apply skills and strategies in reading and writing text).
Step 2: The Coach Teaches the First Lesson
• Using the SFO form and the process described above, the *teacher* observes the Coach, recording examples of the Coach implementing the Observation Focus and how students respond to the instruction.
Step 3: The Teacher Teaches the Second Lesson
• The Coach conducts an SFO, recording instances of the teacher implementing the Observation Focus (with details!) and how students respond.
Step 4: The Coach and Teacher Debrief Together, Reflecting on Their Lessons
• The post-intervention meeting is the most powerful part of the procedure. During this meeting, both the Coach and teacher reflect about their own lessons.   • First, the teacher talks about things he or she noted on the SFO form while the Coach was teaching. During this time, the Coach models self-reflection, revealing that we do not teach perfect lessons and that effective teachers reflect about how they might adjust instruction to make it more effective.   • Next, the Coach talks about the things recorded on the observation form while the teacher was teaching. The Coach leads the teacher through a process of self-reflection about his or her lesson.   • It can be helpful to use the Lesson Reflection form (in the *Appendix*) to provide a framework to guide this debriefing meeting.

which is adapted from a process developed by Showers and Joyce (1996) for their peer-coaching model. This approach incorporates

- co-planning, in which the Coach models lesson planning informed by diagnostic assessments of students' needs;

- modeling instruction;

- observing instruction; and

- modeling self-reflection.

Implementing this process involves four separate time periods: two meetings with the teacher outside of instructional time and two class periods. We describe the procedure in *Table 6.1*. It can be helpful to prepare teachers for this procedure by having them practice using the SFO form and procedure while observing videotapes of effective instruction.

Other Ideas for Making Feedback Less Threatening

The procedures we have described are not appropriate for every situation. The following are some ideas that may make teachers more receptive to a Reading Coach's feedback. Some of these are our ideas, and others came from teachers in our many workshops.

BEFORE THE OBSERVATION

- Ask the teacher what he or she would like you to look for during the observation. Agree on a primary focus.

- Show the teacher any forms and describe any procedures you will use.

- Teach a model lesson and have the teacher observe you using the same form and procedures.

DURING THE OBSERVATION

- Together with the target teacher observe a second teacher and debrief afterward with both of them, with the *observing* teacher providing most of the feedback.

AFTER THE OBSERVATION

- Ask the teacher *why* he or she made certain instructional decisions. There may be a good reason that you don't know about.

- Prioritize and provide feedback on *only one or two* critical things. Imagine that you are working with a struggling reader who makes multiple errors while reading a story. After the reading, you tell the student 15 things to work on. You probably wouldn't expect the student to be able to integrate all that feedback at one time. It's unlikely that the student would be able to apply *any* of your feedback the next time he or she reads a story. Similarly, adults also have problems taking in a lot of feedback at once. Even if you observe a lesson with 15 different problems—or more—it is more helpful to focus on one or two aspects of the lesson. If you met with the teacher before the observation and discussed an Observation Focus, try to limit your feedback to that focus.

- Convey mutual respect. Treat teachers as you would want to be treated: like a valued professional.

- *Always* maintain confidentiality about what you observe. If teachers don't trust you, a healthy coaching relationship will not be possible.

Summary

Reading Coaches are often called upon to conduct classroom observations, but it can be hard to provide teachers with feedback while maintaining collaborative relationships with them. Coaches can avoid some of the feeling of supervision and evaluation by focusing on teacher-student interactions rather than directly on what teachers are doing. Another approach is to conduct two-way observations in which a Coach and teacher co-plan lessons, observe each other, and together reflect about their lessons. The student-focused observation procedures we described in this chapter can help a Coach maintain the attitude of mutual trust and respect that we have found to be so essential to positive coaching experiences.

7

ENGAGING RELUCTANT TEACHERS

Most Reading Coaches find that some teachers are more willing to work with them than others. The purpose of this chapter is to describe some strategies and considerations that may be helpful in establishing positive relationships with teachers who are reluctant to work with a Coach.

Establishing Professional Relationships

Before we begin to think about engaging teachers who are indifferent or even resistant to working with a Reading Coach, it might be helpful to review some important ideas related to defining the coaching role. As we work with Coaches across the country, we find that many of them skipped the fundamental step of clearly defining their roles in their schools. Other Coaches have realized that it's time to return to this discussion with their colleagues and supervisor. When defining the Coach's role, the essential questions to address are the following:

- What is the purpose, the goal, and the rationale for having a Reading Coach?
- What will the Reading Coach do in the school?
- What will the Reading Coach *not* do in the school?

These seem like simple questions, but they lead to important discussions. If the Coach, teachers, and administrators (and, in some cases, district or state representatives) answer these questions differently, there will likely be confusion and tensions around the role of the Coach. If people have different expectations of the coaching role and there are no frank discussions about the situation, someone is bound to be unhappy.

Be sure that the topic of how a Coach can maintain confidentiality with his or her colleagues is a part of this discussion. Many problems can be avoided if administrators will acknowledge—in the presence of the Coach and teachers together—the importance of Coach-teacher confidentiality. Even if the administrators in your school don't make this kind of public statement, an open discussion of issues surrounding confidentiality can have a positive impact on Coach-teacher relationships.

Different Kinds of Teachers

In *The Reading Coach* book, we describe four types of teachers that Coaches are likely to encounter:

- Teachers who are eager for help and open to trying new ideas.

- Teachers who are eager for help but resistant to trying any new strategies.

- Teachers who are not seeking immediate assistance, but are not resistant to the idea of coaching.

- Teachers who are not seeking assistance and are resistant to working with a colleague on classroom issues.

We suggested that the Coach actively work to keep the door open with *all* teachers by checking in with them monthly with three facilitator questions:

1. "What is working well for you?"

2. "Do you have a concern about the progress of any of your students?"

3. "Do you have any questions or suggestions for me?"

We know that it can be challenging to keep going back to a teacher who has made it clear that he or she has no interest in working with you, but we also know that it's nearly impossible to establish a relationship with someone if you never communicate with them. These three questions are generally not threatening, and they may help make a connection that could grow into a professional working relationship.

In this chapter, we describe other ideas for engaging teachers in that fourth category. In particular, we suggest that it can be helpful to try to see the situation from the teacher's point of view, and we'll offer some thoughts about adult change and growth, as well as research on conditions that promote teachers' acceptance and use of educational innovations. Next, we describe a problem-solving approach that may help Coaches take action to work toward more positive relationships. We conclude by summarizing some specific ideas that may help Coaches make positive connections with resistant teachers.

From the Teacher's Point of View

Let's say that you are a Reading Coach and that most of the teachers in your school are working with you at some level on a regular basis, but there are a few teachers who have made it clear that they do not need, or want, your interference in their classrooms. You may feel frustrated, or even somewhat angry, about the situation. Despite these feelings, it can be useful to view the situation from the teachers' point of view. You might begin by honestly asking yourself:

- What may be keeping these teachers from working with the Coach?

- What are the benefits and costs of working with the Coach, from these teachers' point of view?

It may seem odd to think in terms of costs and benefits but analyzing the situation in this way can help a Coach think rationally rather than reacting emotionally to the situation, in much the same way engaging in the Collaborative Planning process puts the focus on *solving* a problem rather than *reacting* to it.

First, let's consider the benefits. From a teacher's point of view, the benefits of working with a Coach might include the following items:

- Improved outcomes for students
- Increased competence and confidence in the ability to provide effective instruction
- More favorable reviews by the principal
- A feeling of being respected and valued as a professional educator
- The social satisfaction of being part of a group that is working toward a common goal

Of course, these benefits might or might not be perceived by the teachers you work with. Part of any strategy to enhance Coach-teacher relationships should include thinking of ways to bring these benefits to the forefront. On the other hand, teachers may perceive potential costs of working with the Coach. Some of the reasons teachers may be resistant include:

- The time demands of attending meetings, planning instruction, preparing for lessons, etc.
- The difficulty of changing teaching practices that may have been implemented for years and a fear of failure in implementing the new practices successfully
- Fear of public embarrassment or humiliation
- Worry that their personal experience and knowledge are not respected
- Fear of their jobs being threatened if the principal thinks they are incompetent
- A reluctance to let go of their current philosophies about reading instruction
- A perception that the Coach bears a political agenda

It may be useful to think specifically about your own situation and about the potential payoffs of the coaching relationship for teachers as well as the risks, fears, and demands. Ask yourself, "What can I do to assure teachers that they will not be humiliated, that I respect them and their experience, and that I will not relay information from our talks or classroom observations to administrators? How can I help these teachers feel more like members of a team with a common goal?" Joyce and Showers (1982) wisely observed that "teachers' lack of interpersonal support and close contact with others in the context of teaching is a tragedy. Coaching reduces this isolation and increases support" (p. 7).

Keep in mind that the most important potential benefit of participating in coaching is *improved outcomes for students*. In fact, research indicates that teachers' perceptions of positive effects on their students will overcome their initial resistance to implementing a practice (Showers et al., 1987). Even if they are philosophically opposed to research-based reading instructional methods, teachers may come to accept these changes if it is clear that the changes result in better outcomes for their students. Showers et al. state that their review of research on professional development indicates that "[i]ndividual teaching styles and value orientations do not often affect teachers' abilities to learn from staff development" and that "a basic level of knowledge or skill in a new approach is necessary *before* teachers can 'buy in' to it" (p. 79).

What are the implications for the Reading Coach? Be sure to make *explicit* the connections between professional development, teachers' actions, and student outcomes, and if student outcomes improve, *give teachers the credit*! Collaboratively examine progress-monitoring data, and *advertise successes* related to coaching.

Some Thoughts About Facilitating Change

Reading Coaches are often given the role of being "change agents" in schools. In fact, the idea of instructional coaching was first developed as a way to give teachers long-term job-embedded support as they learn new ways of teaching. Coaching is a centerpiece in various models of school reform. You may be in a situation in which a major part of your role is to ensure that all teachers implement a new curriculum and/or a set of instructional practices.

The challenge to a Coach in this situation is to promote and inspire positive change without creating an air of superiority, to be a leader but not a supervisor or evaluator. One aspect of the Coach's facilitator role is promoting an open and receptive atmosphere toward change. The Coach can do this by modeling openness to new ideas and by listening thoughtfully and skillfully to colleagues' concerns. There is a saying that captures this idea well: "Be the change you want to see in others."

In an article about change agents in the business world, Recklies (2001) asserts that a good change agent must be able to "take into account the opinions and doubts of others." He explains that successful change agents set clear, realistic goals, but also understand and take into account the existing values, beliefs, and routines of the organization (in this case, the existing school culture). He makes the important observation (p. 1) that:

> Members of the change team and other employees affected by the change initiative must not feel as if they are just the tools for change or the subject of change. In my experience, it is not enough to have a convincing vision. Real commitment can only be gained by giving people the chance to become actively involved, to contribute their own experiences. Every employee needs to know that his contribution to the project is important and is valued. Thus, people will develop a sense of ownership for the project, which, in turn may serve as a major source of motivation when it comes to the inevitable problems and barriers.

Finally, Recklies cites Rosabeth Moss Kanter in his conclusion that the most important qualities a leader can bring to a changing organization are passion, conviction, and confidence in others.

We think this statement from the world of business applies well to successful coaching. Good Coaches have a passion and enthusiasm that is hard to miss, but they also have strong confidence in their colleagues and in the power of collaboration among them. Successful Coaches take care to avoid the "expert" aura. Rather than appearing to be the "source of all answers," they are both teachers *and* learners. Stenger, Tollefson, and Fine (1992) conducted research to learn more about conditions that support teacher participation in educational consultation, an activity similar to coaching. They found that teachers were more likely to participate in consultation when they saw the consultant as a teacher who was just like them but had the benefit of different specialized training. If Coaches actively try to cultivate this attitude, teachers may be more receptive to working with them.

Above all, successful Coaches keep the focus on the students' instructional needs. Coaches, teachers, and administrators meet regularly to examine students' progress monitoring assessment results *without placing blame*, but with an attitude of working together to support every child's growth. This is the strength of Student-Focused Coaching: Teachers and Coaches work *together* to try to figure out ways to support struggling learners. Successful Coaches stress the collaborative nature of coaching and give teachers the credit for successes whenever possible.

Research on Teachers' Use of New Instructional Practices

Gersten, Chard, and Baker (2000) reviewed research on conditions that support teachers' sustained use of research-based instructional practices. Several of their findings have clear implications for the Reading Coach as she or he considers ways to engage reluctant teachers in changing their instructional practices. Some of the important ideas summarized by Gersten et al. are the need to

1. establish realistic plans and expectations for changes in teachers' practices.
2. provide teachers with sufficient time and opportunities to "think through the instructional approach and how it can be used for their students" (p. 457).
3. provide teachers with support systems in the form of "peer networks, … coaching, and joint examination of student data" (p. 457).
4. assure that school administrators provide support for the new practices by, for example, providing release time and funding for necessary materials, rewarding and reinforcing use of the practices, and participating personally in collaborative efforts to support the change process.
5. make explicit and clear the connection between student performance data and the implementation of the change.

Finally, Gersten et al. (2000) caution that leaders who want to promote the sustained use of research-based practices should "move slowly enough to ensure quality" (p. 457). The authors suggest that real change typically takes time, citing research demonstrating that it may take teachers as long as two years to truly master a new practice, and they caution against introducing too many new strategies or approaches over the course of one school year. Gersten et al. also emphasize the necessity that teachers not only learn *how to perform* the new practices, but that they develop a *real understanding* and *confidence* in their abilities to implement them.

In general, teachers who have the *time, resources,* and *support* they need to become *truly competent and confident* in the implementation of new practices are more likely to implement and sustain those practices (Gersten et al., 2000; Showers et al., 1987), especially when they perceive those practices as feasible in the realities of the classroom. Gersten and colleagues (2000) suggest that most teachers are open to learning new practices as long as these practices are feasible, and that those providing professional development understand the reality that classrooms are very complex environments and that many factors can affect the use and effects of instructional practices.

Some practical implications for the Coach, particularly when working with teachers who are not enthusiastic about the experience, are to introduce new practices so that they will not require large changes at one time. Remember that teachers are most likely to adopt new practices when they are practical, manageable, and not overly demanding of time (for planning or instruction). To kick-start the process, think about asking teachers to implement practices that require a small investment of time and energy, but that are likely to have effects that show up in progress monitoring. For example, perhaps you could show kindergarten teachers how they can implement 10–15 minutes of game-like phonological awareness practice each day while students are waiting in line or during transition times. Or maybe fifth grade teachers could learn to teach their students a partner-reading routine and to provide 20 minutes each day for repeated oral reading in pairs. The kindergarten intervention may result in improved outcomes on assessments of phonemic awareness, and the fifth grade activity may result in improved fluency scores. If these results do emerge, be sure to point out the connection between the simple practices teachers implemented and the improved student outcomes.

A Problem-Solving Approach

Regardless of our profession, from time to time each of us has to work with people whom we find difficult. The challenge of team building in the world of business has resulted in a lot of discussion and writing about working with "difficult people." Reading Coaches may find it helpful to review the statements in *Table 7.1* (Mudore, 2001) and their implications for working with teachers who are not open to coaching.

With these statements in mind, we suggest that Coaches engage in a problem-solving process if they have serious difficulties working with certain teachers. The Coach should think about behaviors that he or she *can* change to move the situation forward. If possible, it may be helpful to review the situation with a fellow Coach, but remember that your relationship with

Table 7.1 **Central Ideas Related to Working with "Difficult" People**

You cannot change other people.
The only thing you can change is your own behavior and the way you respond to them.
Wishing they were different won't change the situation.
It is not about winning or losing.

your teacher colleagues is confidential; do not use any teachers' names or share other identifying information. You can follow a process similar to what you do when problem solving in relation to a student's reading progress. However, if you do not have a fellow Coach or someone else with whom you can collaborate, you can think through each step on your own.

First, define the problem and set goals. Let's say that you have a somewhat strained relationship with Mrs. Green, a third grade classroom teacher who has taught in the same school for the past 23 years. As you address the issue, take care that you don't confuse the *person* and the *problem*. Mrs. Green is not "a problem," but your relationship with her may be problematic. It may be helpful to consider the topics we discussed earlier in this chapter. Try to think about the problem from the teacher's point of view. What are the "costs" to the teacher of working with the Coach? Think about the characteristics of human growth and change and the conditions that make it more likely that teachers will adopt and sustain new practices. Are there any other factors you can identify that may be contributing to the problem? Remember to do a little soul-searching here. For example, could part of the problem be that the Coach (you!) is a close long-time friend of one of the other third-grade teachers and that Mrs. Green is afraid the Coach and the other teacher will discuss Mrs. Green behind her back? Is there something you can do to establish more professional relationships with your colleagues (or at least discuss the nature of these professional relationships)?

You will probably be able to develop a hypothesis regarding the real problem, although it may be difficult or impossible to gather data to test this hypothesis unless you ask Mrs. Green about her feelings. Let's say, in our scenario, that you hypothesize that Mrs. Green doesn't want to work with a Reading Coach because she thinks that it will be very demanding on her time. She has been teaching reading in pretty much the same way for several years, and changing would take extra planning, preparation of materials, etc. Mrs. Green may also feel that her years of experience are not valued since everyone is talking about change all the time. On the other hand, she may be afraid that she might not be able to learn the new methods and that the principal will find out that she's an "old dog" who can't learn "new tricks."

The next step is to set a goal for your work with Mrs. Green. If she has refused to work with you at all, it is probably not wise to aim for all-out collaboration right off the bat. Think about a focused, meaningful goal. Remember that it has to be observable and measureable. In our scenario, you might set the goal that Mrs. Green will engage in a co-planning session with you along with other third grade teachers. Or maybe you could have the goal that she will agree to observe a fellow teacher who is implementing the new curriculum.

Your "intervention plan" for your relationship with Mrs. Green will probably be strongly linked to the goal, but it may include intermediate steps leading to the goal. For example, you might start by setting up a regular co-planning session to which all the third grade teachers are invited, and be sure that Mrs. Green knows she is invited to attend. You may offer to help teachers who attend the co-planning sessions develop or find any resources or materials they may need to implement their plans. Word may get back to Mrs. Green and she may be enticed by her colleagues to attend the sessions.

If your goal is that Mrs. Green will observe and debrief with another teacher who is successfully implementing new research-supported practices in his or her reading instruction, you may set up a peer observation initiative in which teachers in several grades are paired and observe each other. If you do this, be sure to pair teachers with less experience and success implementing new approaches with other teachers who have more experience and expertise. You may also pair a teacher who is reluctant to work with the Coach with one who has worked with you frequently and experienced benefits from the collaboration. In these pairs, we suggest that you have them follow the two-way observation process we described in Chapter 6, "Student-Focused Classroom Observations." This process was developed specifically for peer coaching by Showers and Joyce (1996).

Next, determine how the plan will be monitored and evaluated. This will again be closely linked to the goal. You might simply track Mrs. Green's attendance at co-planning meetings or the number of times she works with her peer-coaching partner. Of course, the next step is to implement the plan and monitor progress toward the goal. After a reasonable period of time, evaluate the success of the plan and decide whether you will continue it, change it, or set a new goal.

A Few More Ideas

Table 7.2 summarizes some of the ideas presented in this chapter and others from various sources, including participants in our workshops. This list is certainly not exhaustive; you and your fellow Coaches will probably be able to add to it. Engaging in this kind of planning and problem solving is an important part of coaching in most schools. We hope that some of these ideas may help you start that process.

Summary and Conclusion

In this chapter we've suggested some "food for thought" and a few ideas that may help a Coach establish a working relationship with a resistant teacher. Clearly, there are no easy answers, and we know the frustration of trying to work with people who are not interested in working with you. Our best advice is to keep working at the relationships, keep coming back with the facilitator questions we provided (and others you may think of yourself), and problem-solve with a trusted colleague. Keep in mind that we truly cannot change other

Table 7.2 **Promoting Teacher Participation in Coaching**

- Review ideas in *The Reading Coach* book about establishing professional relationships.
- Use the three facilitator questions at least once per month with every teacher.
- Continue to have open and frank discussions about the coaching role, professional relationships, and confidentiality with all participants.
- Think about each situation from the teacher's point of view. Think about ways to highlight the potential benefits and address the potential costs of working with the Coach.
- Think of ways you can convey your respect for teachers. Treat teachers as valued professionals and try to reduce the "expert" aura.
- Keep the focus on the students' instructional needs rather than teachers' weaknesses.
- Work on enhancing your communication skills—especially listening skills.
- Consider peer coaching (e.g., pairing teachers and using the two-way observation approach described in Chapter 6, "Student-Focused Classroom Observations").
- Be one of the team. Volunteer for duties and attend faculty meetings.
- Ask teachers what topics they would like you to address in professional development, and then be sure to respond to the needs that teachers express.
- Establish and make explicit links between teacher and student needs, professional development and coaching, and student outcomes.
- Examine assessment data with teachers in a collaborative, non-judgmental way and help teachers clarify their needs.
- Give teachers the credit when students make progress.
- Keep advertising; share success stories publicly.
- Give teachers feedback about the results of new practices they have used.
- Don't try to change too much too soon.
- Introduce new practices that are practical and not overly demanding of teachers' time and energy, but that are likely to result in observable student improvement.
- Think about what you can change in your own behaviors and relationships that may make it less threatening for teachers to work with you.
- Remember the three keys to bringing about change in any organization: passion, commitment, and confidence in others. Cultivate these attitudes and communicate them to your colleagues.

people and that wishing they were different is a waste of time and energy. All we can do is consider the things that we *can* change that may help overcome obstacles and encourage our colleagues to work with us. There's a very good reason to do this, of course—all the many students that these teachers are working with now and will work with in the future.

Our hearts are with you, Reading Coaches. We know it's not always easy, but we hope you know how important you are. You truly make a difference for many, many struggling students. **Thank you** for all that you do!

REFERENCES

CHAPTER 1

Bean, R. M., & Zigmond, N. (2006). *Professional development role of reading coaches: In and out of the classroom.* Paper presented at the IRA Reading Research Conference, Chicago, Illinois.

Costa, A., & Garmston, R. (1997). *Cognitive coaching: A foundation for renaissance schools* (3rd ed.). Norwood, MA: Christopher-Gordon.

Darling-Hammond, L., & McLaughlin, M. W. (1996). Policies that support professional development in an era of reform. In M. W. McLaughlin & I. Oberman (Eds.), *Teacher learning: New policy, new practices* (pp. 202–218). New York: Teachers College Press.

Erchul, W. P., & Sheridan, S. M. (Eds.) (2007). *Handbook of research in school psychology.* Mahwah, NJ: Erlbaum.

Hasbrouck, J., & Denton, C. (2005). *The reading coach: A how-to manual for success.* Longmont, CO: Sopris West Educational Services.

Kampwirth, T. J. (2006). *Collaborative consultation in the schools.* Upper Saddle River, NJ: Merrill.

Showers, B., & Joyce, B. (1996). The evolution of peer coaching. *Educational Leaadership, 53*(6), 12–16.

Sugai, G. M., & Tindal, G. A. (1993). *Effective school consultation: An interactive approach.* Pacific Grove, CA: Brooks/Cole.

CHAPTER 2

Denton, C. A., Foorman, B. R., & Mathes, P. M. (2003). Schools that "beat the odds": Implications for reading instruction. *Remedial and Special Education, 24,* 258–261.

Elbaum, B., Vaughn, S., Hughes, M. T., & Moody, S. W. (2000). How effective are one-to-one tutoring programs in reading for elementary students at risk for reading failure? *Journal of Educational Psychology, 92*(4), 605–619.

Fletcher, J. M., Denton, C. A., Fuchs, L., & Vaughn, S. R. (2005). Multi-tiered reading instruction: Linking general education and special education. In International Reading Association, S. O. Richardson & J. W. Gilger (Eds.), *Research-based education and intervention: What we need to know* (pp. 21–43). Baltimore: Author.

Fletcher, J. M., Lyon, G. R., Fuchs, L. S., & Barnes, M. A. (2007). *Learning disabilities: From identification to intervention.* New York: Guilford Press.

Foorman, B. R., Francis, D. J., Fletcher, J. M., Schatschneider, C., & Mehta, P. (1998). The role of instruction in learning to read: Preventing reading disabilities in at-risk children. *Journal of Educational Psychology, 90,* 37–55.

Francis, D. J., Shaywitz, S. E., Stuebing, K. K., Shaywitz, B. A., & Fletcher, J. M. (1996). Developmental lag versus deficit models of reading disability: A longitudinal, individual growth curves analysis. *Journal of Educational Psychology, 88,* 3–17.

Grek, M. L., Mathes, P. G., & Torgesen, J. K. (2003). Similarities and differences between experienced teachers and trained paraprofessionals. In S. Vaughn & K. L. Briggs (Eds.), *Reading in the classroom: Systems for the observation of teaching and learning* (pp. 267–296). Baltimore: Paul H. Brookes.

Haager, D., Klingner, J., & Vaughn, S. (2007). *Evidence-based reading practices for response to intervention.* Baltimore: Paul H. Brookes.

Juel, C. (1988). Learning to read and write: A longitudinal study of 54 children from first through fourth grades. *Journal of Educational Psychology, 80,* 437–447.

Snow, C. E., Burns, M. S., & Griffin, P. (Eds.). (1998). *Preventing reading difficulties in young children.* Report of the National Research Council. Washington, DC: National Academy Press.

Stanovich, K. E. (1986). Matthew effects in reading: Some consequences of individual differences in the acquisition of literacy. *Reading Research Quarterly, 21,* 360–407.

Torgesen, J. K. (1998). Catch them before they fall: Identification and assessment to prevent reading failure in young children. *American Educator, 22,* 1–8. Retrieved August 4, 2008, from http://www.aft.org/pubs-reports/american_educator/spring_sum98/torgesen.pdf

Torgesen, J. K., & Burgess, S. R. (1998). Consistency of reading-related phonological processes throughout early childhood: Evidence from longitudinal-correlational and instructional studies. In J. Metsala & L. Ehri (Eds.), *Word recognition in beginning reading.* Hillsdale, NJ: Erlbaum.

Vaughn, S., & Linan-Thompson, S. (2003). Group size and time allotted to intervention: Effects for students with reading difficulties. In B. Foorman (Ed.), *Preventing and remediating reading difficulties: Bringing science to scale* (pp. 275–298). Baltimore: York.

CHAPTER 3

Sprick, R., Booher, M., & Garrison, M. (2009). *B-RTI: Behavioral response to intervention: Creating a continuum of problem-solving and support.* Eugene, OR: Pacific Northwest Publishing.

Sprick, R., & Garrison, M. (2008). *Interventions: Evidence-based behavioral strategies for individual students* (2nd ed.). Eugene, OR: Pacific Northwest Publishing.

Sprick, R., Sprick, M., & Garrison, M. (1993). *Interventions: Collaborative planning for students at risk.* Longmont, CO: Sopris West Educational Services.

CHAPTER 4

Bryant, D. P., & Bryant, B. R. (2003). *Assistive technology for individuals with disabilities.* Boston: Allyn and Bacon.

Bryant, D. P., Smith, D. D., & Bryant, B. R. (2008). *Teaching students with special needs in inclusive classrooms.* Boston: Allyn and Bacon.

Denton, C. A., & Hocker, J. L. (2006). *Responsive reading instruction: Flexible intervention for struggling readers in the early grades.* Longmont, CO: Sopris West Educational Services.

Foorman, B. R., Francis, D. J., Fletcher, J. M., Schatschneider, C., & Mehta, P. (1998). The role of instruction in learning to read: Preventing reading failure in at-risk children. *Journal of Educational Psychology, 90,* 38–55.

CHAPTER 5

Council for Exceptional Children. (2003). *What every special educator must know: Ethics, standards, and guidelines for special educators* (5th ed.). Arlington, VA: Author.

Dole, J. (2004). The changing role of the reading specialist in school reform. *The Reading Teacher, (57)*5, 462–471.

Gibson, V., & Hasbrouck, J. (2008). *Differentiated instruction: Grouping for success.* New York: McGraw-Hill Higher Education.

National Education Association (NEA). (1975). Code of ethics of the education profession. Retrieved August 4, 2008, from http://www.nea.org/aboutnea/code.html

Office of Special Education Programs (OSEP). *Technical Assistance (TA) Center on school-wide positive behavioral interventions and supports.* U.S. Department of Education. Undated brochure. Retrieved August 4, 2008, from http://www.pbis.org/files/brochure.pdf

Sprick, R., Booher, M., & Garrison, M. (2009). *B-RTI: Behavioral response to intervention: Creating a continuum of problem-solving and support.* Eugene, OR: Pacific Northwest Publishing.

Sprick, R., & Garrison, M. (2008). *Interventions: Evidence-based behavioral strategies for individual students* (2nd ed.). Eugene, OR: Pacific Northwest Publishing.

Sprick, R. S., Garrison, M., & Howard, L. S. (1998). *CHAMPs: A proactive and positive approach to classroom management.* Eugene, OR: Pacific Northwest Publishing.

Sugai, G., & Horner, R. (2007). *Is school-wide positive behavior support an evidence-based practice?* Eugene, OR: OSEP Center on Positive Behavioral Interventions and Supports.

CHAPTER 6

Joyce, B. R., & Showers, B. (1981). Transfer of training: The contribution of "coaching." *Journal of Education, 163*(2), 163–172.

Joyce, B., & Showers, B. (1982). The coaching of teaching. *Educational Leadership, 40,* (2), 4–8, 10.

Showers, B., & Joyce, B. (1996). The evolution of peer coaching. *Educational Leadership, 53,* 12–16.

CHAPTER 7

Gersten, R., Chard, D., & Baker, S. (2000). Factors enhancing sustained use of research-based instructional practices. *Journal of Learning Disabilities, 33,* 445–457.

Mudore, F. (2001). Working with difficult people. *Career World.* Weekly Reader group. Retrieved August 4, 2008, from http://findarticles.com/p/articles/mi_m0HUVis_5_29/ai_70652216/print

Recklies, D. (2001). *What makes a good change agent?* Recklies Management Project. Retrieved August 4, 2008, from http://www.themanager.org/Strategy/change_agent.htm

Showers, B., & Joyce, B. (1996). The evolution of peer coaching. *Educational Leadership, 53,* 12–16.

Showers, B., Joyce, B., & Bennett, B. (1987). Synthesis of research on staff development: A framework for future study and a state-of-the-art analysis. *Educational Leadership, 45,* 77–87.

Stenger, M. K., Tollefson, N., & Fine, M. J. (1992). Variables that distinguish elementary teachers who participate in school-based consultation from those who do not. *School Psychology Quarterly, 7,* 271–284.

RESOURCES FOR THE READING COACH

WEB RESOURCES

Center for Effective Collaboration and Practice (CECP): http://cecp.air.org

Office of Special Education Programs (OSEP), Technical Assistance Center on Positive Behavioral Interventions & Supports (PBIS): http://www.pbis.org

Safe & Civil Schools: http://www.safeandcivilschools.com

BOOKS AND ARTICLES

Abbott, S. P., & Berninger, V. W. (1999). It's never too late to remediate: Teaching word recognition to students with reading disabilities in grades 4–7. *Annals of Dyslexia, 49*, 223–250.

Algozzine, R., & Kay, P. (Eds.). (2002). *Preventing problem behaviors: A handbook of successful prevention strategies.* Thousand Oaks, CA: Corwin Press.

Beck, R. (1997–2004). *RIDE: Responding to individual differences in education.* Longmont, CO: Sopris West Educational Services.

Blachman, B. A., Schatschneider, C., Fletcher, J. M., Francis, D. J., Clonan, S., Shaywitz, B., & Shaywitz, S. (2004). Effects of intensive reading remediation for second and third graders. *Journal of Educational Psychology, 96*, 444- 461.

Bryant, D.P., Goodwin, M., Bryant, B.R., & Higgins, K. (2003). Vocabulary instruction for students with learning disabilities: A review of the research. *Learning Disability Quarterly, 26*(2), 117-128.

Cotton, K. (2000). *Schooling practices that matter most.* Portland, OR: Northwest Regional Education Laboratory.

Curtis, M. (2004). Adolescents who struggling with word identification: Research and Practice. In T.L. Jetton & J.A. Dole (Eds.) *Adolescent literacy research and practice* (119-134). New York: Guilford.

Denton, C.A., Fletcher, J. M., Simos, P.C., Papanicolaou, A.C. & Anthony, J.L. (2007). An implementation of a tiered intervention model: Reading outcomes and neural correlates. In D. Haager, J., Klingner, & S. Vaughn (Eds.). *Evidence-based reading practices for response to intervention* (pp. 107-137). Baltimore, MD: Brookes.

Denton, C.A., & Hocker, J.L. (2006). *Responsive reading instruction: Flexible intervention for struggling readers in the early grades.* Longmont, CO: Sopris West.

Denton, C.A., & Mathes, P.G. (2003). Intervention for Struggling Readers: Possibilities and Challenges. In B.R. Foorman (Ed.), *Preventing and Remediating Reading Difficulties: Bringing Science to Scale* (pp. 229-251). Timonium, MD: York Press.

Ebbers, S., and Denton, C.A. (2008). A Root Awakening: Effective Vocabulary Instruction for Older Students with Reading Difficulties. *Learning Disabilities Research and Practice. 23*(2), 90-102.

Elbaum, B., Vaughn, S., Hughes, M. T., & Moody, S. W. (2000). How effective are one-to-one tutoring programs in reading for elementary students at risk for reading failure? *Journal of Educational Psychology, 92*(4), 605–619.

Fletcher, J.M., Denton, C.A., Fuchs, L., & Vaughn, S.R. (2005). Multi-tiered reading instruction: Linking general education and special education. In International Reading Association, S.O. Richardson & J.W. Gilger (Eds.), *Research-Based Education and Intervention: What We Need to Know* (pp. 21-43). Baltimore: Author.

Foorman, B. R. (Ed.) (2003). *Preventing and Remediating Reading Difficulties: Bringing Science to Scale.* Timonium, MD: York Press.Gersten, R., Fuchs, L., Williams, J., & Baker, S. (2001). Teaching reading comprehension strategies to students with learning disabilities: A review of research. Review of Educational Research, 71, 279–320.

Grek, M. L., Mathes, P. G., & Torgesen, J. K. (2003). Similarities and differences between experienced teachers and trained paraprofessionals. In S. Vaughn & K. L. Briggs (Eds.), *Reading in the classroom: Systems for the observation of teaching and learning* (pp. 267–296). Baltimore: Brookes.

Gibson, V., & Hasbrouck, J. (2007). *Differentiated Instruction: Grouping for Success.* NY: McGraw Hill Higher Education.

Haager, D., Klingner, J., & Vaughn, S. (Eds.) (2007). *Evidence-based reading practices for response to intervention.* Baltimore, MD: Brookes.

International Dyslexia Association (2005). *Research-Based Education and Intervention: What We Need to Know.* Baltimore: Author.

Horner, R., & Sugai, G. (2007). *Evidence based research on school-wide positive behavior support.* Retrieved August 4, 2008, from http://www.pbis.org/researchLiterature.htm#s

Jenson, W. R., Rhode, G., Evans, C., Reavis, K., Morgan, D. P., Sheridan, S., et al. *The tough kid® series.* Longmont, CO: Sopris West Educational Services.

Jimmerson, S.R., Burns, M.K., & VanDerHeyden, A.M. (Eds.) (2007). *Handbook of response to intervention: The science and practice of assessment and intervention*. New York: Springer.

Jitendra, A., Edwards, L., Sacks, G., & Jacobson, L. (2004). What research says about vocabulary instruction for students with learning disabilities. *Exceptional Children, 70*, 299-311.

Kame'enui, E. J., & Darch, C. B. (2004). *Instructional classroom management: A proactive approach to behavior management* (2nd ed.). White Plains, NY: Longman.

Kerr, M. M., & Nelson, C. M. (2002). *Strategies for addressing behavior problems in the classroom*. Upper Saddle River, NJ: Merrill.

Mathes, P. G., & Denton, C.A. (2002). The prevention and identification of reading disability. *Seminars in Pediatric Neurology, 9*(3), 185-191.

McMaster, K.L., Fuchs, D., & Fuchs, L.S. (2006). Research on peer-assisted learning strategies: The promise and limitations of peer-mediated instruction. *Reading & Writing Quarterly, 22*, 5-25.

McMaster, K. L., Fuchs, D., Fuchs, L. S., & Compton, D. L. (2005). Responding to nonresponders: An experimental field trial of identification and intervention methods. *Exceptional Children, 71*(4), 445–463.

Saenz, L.M., Fuchs, L.S., & Fuchs, D. (2005). Peer-assisted learning strategies for English language learners with learning disabilities. *Exceptional Children, 71*, 231-247.

Scammacca, N., Roberts, G., Vaughn. S., Edmonds, M., Wexler, J., Reutebuch, C. K., & Torgesen, J. K. (2007). *Interventions for adolescent struggling readers: A meta-analysis with implications for practice*. Portsmouth, NH: RMC Research Corporation, Center on Instruction.

Sprague, J., & Golly, A. (2004). *Best behavior book: Building positive behavior support in schools*. Longmont, CO: Sopris West Educational Services.

Sprick, R. S. (2006). *Discipline in the secondary classroom: A positive approach to behavior management*. Eugene, OR: Pacific Northwest Publishing.

Sprick, R., Booher, M., & Garrison, M. (2009). *B-RTI: Behavioral response to intervention: Creating a continuum of problem-solving and support*. Eugene, OR: Pacific Northwest Publishing.

Sprick, R. S., & Garrison, M. (2008). *Interventions: Evidence-based behavior strategies for individual students*. Eugene, OR: Pacific Northwest Publishing.

Sprick, R. S., Garrison, M., & Howard, L. S. (1998). *CHAMPs: A proactive and positive approach to classroom management*. Eugene, OR: Pacific Northwest Publishing.

Sprick, R. S., & Howard, L. (2000). *Teacher's encyclopedia of behavior management: 100 problems/ 500 plans*. Eugene, OR: Pacific Northwest Publishing.

Sprick, R. S., Howard, L., Wise, B. J., Marcum, K., & Haykin, M. (1998). *The administrator's desk reference of behavior management* (vols. 1–3). Eugene, OR: Pacific Northwest Publishing.

Sprick, R. S., Knight, J., Reinke, W., & McKale, T. (2007). *Coaching classroom management.* Eugene, OR: Pacific Northwest Publishing.

Tindal, G., Hasbrouck, J., & Jones, C. (2005). *Oral reading fluency: 90 years of measurement.* (Technical Report No. 33, Behavioral Research and Teaching). Eugene, OR: University of Oregon.

Torgesen, J.K. (1998). Catch them before they fall: Identification and assessment to prevent reading failure in young children. *American Educator, 22*, 1-8. Retrieved on November 7, 2007 from www.aft.org/pubs-reports/american_educator/spring_sum98/torgesen.pdf

Torgesen, J. K. (2000). Individual differences in response to early interventions in reading: The lingering problem of treatment resisters. *Learning Disabilities Research & Practice, 15*, 55–64.

Vaughn, S., Fletcher, J.M., Francis. D.J., Denton, C.A., Wanzek, J., Cirino, P., Barth, A., & Romain, M. (2008). Response to intervention with older students with reading difficulties. *Learning and Individual Differences, 18*, 338-345.

Vaughn, S., & Fuchs, L. S., (2003). Redefining learning disabilities as inadequate response to treatment: The promise and potential problems. *Learning Disabilities Research & Practice, 18*(3), 137–146.

Vaughn, S., & Linan-Thompson, S. (2004). *Research-based methods of reading instruction: Grades K-3.* Alexandria, VA: Association for Supervision and Curriculum Development.

Walker, H., Colvin, G., & Ramsey, E. (1995). *Antisocial behavior in public school: Strategies and best practices.* Pacific Grove, CA: Brooks/Cole.

JOURNALS

Behavioral Disorders: http://www.ccbd.net/behavioraldisorders/Journal/index.cfm

Journal of Emotional and Behavioral Disorders: http://ebx.sagepub.com/

Journal of Evidence-Based Practices for Schools: http://www.rowmaneducation.com/journals/JEBP/

Journal of Positive Behavior Interventions: http://pbi.sagepub.com/

The Journal of Special Education: http://sed.sagepub.com/

APPENDIX

Student-Focused Observation Form

Teacher _____ Grade or Class _____ Date _____

Coach _____ Start Time _____ End Time _____

Observation Focus _____

Teacher Behaviors	Student Behaviors

Summary and Comments

Lesson Reflection Form

Lesson Reflection	
What were my goals?	**What happened in the lesson?**
What should I change?	**What should stay the same?**
What's the plan?	

The 25-Minute Process for BEHAVIOR CONCERNS

PRIOR TO MEETING

- Contact parent(s) or guardian(s) as school policy or situation requires.

STEP 1: BACKGROUND (6 MINUTES)

- *Describe* the problem(s) by identifying when, where, how often, how long, etc., the problem occurs.
- Identify the student's *strengths*.
- Identify the *strategies* that have already been tried.

STEP 2: PROBLEM AND GOAL (2 MINUTES)

- *Narrow the scope* of the problem and identify a goal.

STEP 3: CORRECTIVE CONSEQUENCES (2 MINUTES)

- Determine whether irresponsible or inappropriate behavior will be *corrected, ignored,* or a *consequence* will be implemented.

STEP 4: RESPONSIBLE AND IRRESPONSIBLE BEHAVIOR (4 MINUTES)

- Provide *examples* of responsible behavior and/or student strengths to encourage *as well as* irresponsible/inappropriate behavior to discourage.

STEP 5: PROACTIVE STRATEGIES (4 MINUTES) (*DO NOT* EVALUATE.)

- Brainstorm strategies to encourage responsible behavior.

STEP 6: CREATE THE PLAN (3 MINUTES)

- The teacher(s) selects a manageable set of proactive strategies to implement.

STEP 7: FINAL DETAILS (4 MINUTES)

a. *Evaluation*:

- Identify at least two ways to determine if the plan is working.

b. *Support*:

- Identify what other adults can do to assist the student and the teacher(s). Be specific—who, what, where, when.

c. *Plan summary*:

- Identify each person's responsibilities and when actions will be taken.
- Identify who will discuss the plan with the student and when.
- Schedule follow-up meeting.

Adapted from Sprick, R., Booher, M., & Garrison, M. (2009). *B-RTI: Behavioral response to intervention: Creating a continuum of problem-solving and support.* Eugene, OR: Pacific Northwest Publishing.

The 25-Minute Process for ACADEMIC CONCERNS

PRIOR TO MEETING
- Conduct informal assessments (including IRI/oral reading fluency checks).
- Analyze student's work samples.
- Work 1:1 with the student on an assignment.
- Review student's repertoire of school success strategies (e.g., note-taking, test-taking, study skills, organizational strategies).
- Contact parent(s) or guardian(s) as school policy or situation requires.

STEP 1: BACKGROUND (6 MINUTES)
- *Describe/present* the academic problem using collected information.
  (If more information is needed, *stop here* and reschedule the meeting.)
- Describe the student's academic *strengths* and *needs* based on gathered information.

STEP 2: PROBLEM AND GOAL (3 MINUTES)
- Target *specific areas* that require assistance (i.e., instruction, remediation/intervention, accommodations).
- Discuss *goals* for improvement.

STEP 3: STRATEGIES (8 MINUTES)
Do not evaluate. Review and brainstorm:
- Classroom adaptations (e.g., classroom structure and organization, presentation of information, use of written assignments, structured grading systems).
- Adaptive accommodations (e.g., highlighting, use of audiotapes, study buddies, reduced workload).
- Instruction and remediation/interventions to improve the student's skills and strategies.

STEP 4: CREATE THE PLAN (5 MINUTES)
- The teacher(s) selects a manageable set of strategies to implement.

STEP 5: FINAL DETAILS (3 MINUTES)
a. *Evaluation*:
- Identify at least two ways to determine if the plan is working.
b. *Support*:
- Identify what other adults can do to assist the student and the teacher(s). Be specific—who, what, where, when.
c. *Plan a summary*:
- Identify each person's responsibilities and when actions will be taken.
- Identify who will discuss the plan with the student and when.
- Schedule follow-up meeting.

Adapted from Sprick, R., Booher, M., & Garrison, M. (2009). *B-RTI: Behavioral response to intervention: Creating a continuum of problem-solving and support.* Eugene, OR: Pacific Northwest Publishing.

Group Problem-Solving Timelines

STRUCTURED INTERVENTION PLANNING FOR **BEHAVIOR**	25 minutes	35 minutes	50 minutes
Step 1 BACKGROUND	6	7	10
Step 2 PROBLEM & GOAL	2	3	4
Step 3 CORRECTIVE CONSEQUENCES	2	3	4
Step 4 RESPONSIBLE & IRRESPONSIBLE BEHAVIOR	4	6	8
Step 5 PROACTIVE STRATEGIES	4	6	8
Step 6 PROACTIVE PLAN	3	4	8
Step 7 FINAL DETAILS	4	6	8

STRUCTURED INTERVENTION PLANNING FOR **ACADEMICS**	25 minutes	35 minutes	50 minutes
Step 1 BACKGROUND	6	8	10
Step 2 PROBLEM & GOAL	3	5	9
Step 3 PROACTIVE STRATEGIES	8	10	12
Step 4 CREATE THE PLAN	5	7	10
Step 5 FINAL DETAILS	3	5	9